Super Sewing
Series

MARJORIE ARCH BURNS

THE SHIRT LOOK

J. B. LIPPINCOTT COMPANY PHILADELPHIA/NEW YORK/SAN JOSE

Printed in the United States of America
ISBN 0-397-40193-0
BICENTENNIAL EDITION

Book design, art, and cover: Ann Atene

This book contains some of the basic principles of the Bishop
Method of Clothing Construction from the original texts.

15.7512.1

THE SHIRT LOOK
by Marjorie Arch Burns
Super Sewing Series

THE ADAPTABLE SHIRT   The classic shirt always has a place in fashion. This easy-to-wear, adaptable, flattering garment has never been more popular. It appears in a variety of garments for day and evening wear. Women have found a new interest in the shirt dress, soft or tailored. Shirts and shirt jackets are good with pants. Men's fashions include shirt suits and shirt jackets.

This book offers a variety of construction details that cannot be found in pattern instruction sheets. These will help you achieve all kinds of shirt looks, using, perhaps, only one pattern. You will learn how to adjust your pattern and custom-fit it. Once this has been done and you have mastered the easy techniques for making the details of superior quality that are given in this book, you can make a shirt in an evening.

Treat yourself to a wardrobe of shirts. Vary the details (sleeve length, collars, cuffs, shirtbands, polo openings, pockets, buttons) with the fabric to achieve a particular look. For work, try a pants suit in gabardine. Shirt jacket and pants in matching heavy and lightweight denim combine to make a great look for active out-door sports. A large shirt gives good protection from the sun when worn over a swimsuit as a beach coverup. Add a bold, attention-getting appliqué for trim. For an attractive at-home look, sew a shirt-to-the-floor in a soft, clingy knit. For a morale lift in the warm-weather doldrums, what about a sleeveless shirt dress of crisp linen in a luscious ice-cream color? Make a gauzy shirt to wear over flare-leg pajamas or a sweeping skirt for a smashing evening look.

Make a suede or bold, blanket-plaid shirt jacket for the man in your life. Sew him a corduroy shirt suit. Or give him this book — he might enjoy making one of these himself. With shirts the only limit is your own imagination. Turn the page, and Open Sesame!

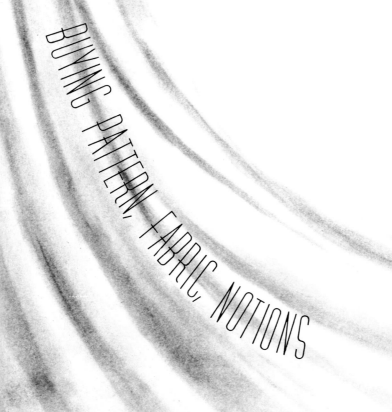

PATTERN

While many kinds of garments can have the shirt look, the look it-self can include variations in style. For example, a shirt-style jacket normally has a shirt collar, a front-buttoned opening, and shirt-style sleeves, but it can be designed straight and undarted, with a fitted waist, or with a tunnel belt. The collar may be rounded or pointed; it may or may not have a separate neckband. The sleeves may be long or short. When you choose your pattern, make sure the design is flattering to you. There is such a variety to choose from, you are sure to find the look that is you. For even greater choice, you can learn to combine two or more patterns.

In order to make a really good-looking garment, you must con-sider your figure as well as your taste. If you know from experi-ence that your shoulders are difficult to fit, do not buy a shirt pat-tern with a yoke and no shoulder seams. It would be hard to alter.

Pay special attention to the collar style. While the outside edges of a collar can be changed to suit you and your fabric, the whole should be in proportion to your face and figure. Study the way the collar lies in the pattern illustration to see if it will look well on you.

BUYING PATTERN, FABRIC, NOTIONS

You will also find that a collar with a neckband cut separately will look and fit better than a collar cut in one with the neckband. The two-piece construction is more complex, but the better fit will make your efforts worthwhile.

Finally, there are other design details you may want in a pattern. Many of these may be added with the instructions in this book. A woman with a B or C bust cup will need a bust dart in a shirt-style garment just as she does in any other garment. Very few shirt patterns provide a bust dart, and it is more important to buy a pattern that has the yoke, collar, sleeves, or other details you want. Instructions for adding a bust dart to a pattern are given in Finding the Perfect Fit, page 99.

In Custom Looks, learn how to add side openings to a shirt designed without them and how to curve openings that are straight. You will also find ways to vary pockets, plackets, cuffs, and other details. The most important thing to look for, then, in choosing a pattern is the shape you like: the overall shape of the garment; a fitted waist, if desired; easily fitted shoulders when shoulders are a problem area; and a collar that lies in a way that flatters your face.

For women, patterns for the shirt look should be purchased by the bust size in the proper figure type. To measure, place tape over the apex (fullest part) of the bust and straight across the back.

For men, a shirt or shirt jacket pattern should be chosen by the chest size in the proper figure type. To measure, place the tape measure straight around at the fullest part of the chest.

FABRIC SELECTION

Take time to select your fabric. The back of the pattern envelope will tell you what fabrics are suitable for the pattern. When you find a fabric you like, inspect it carefully, feeling it to decide if it has the qualities you want for the shirt look you will make. You should be able to tell if it is suited to crisp, clean lines or if it would be better for a close-fitting shirt or for a shirt blouse. If your pattern has a yoke and you are choosing a fairly heavy fabric for your garment, you may want to purchase a lightweight fabric for the yoke facing.

7

While the pattern envelope may limit you to a certain weight or category of fabric (stable or stretchy), it never limits the type of fabric you may choose. The length can be adjusted to make a shirt or jacket and, for women, a dress or floor-length dress.

Combinations of Fabrics   Make the yoke from contrasting fabric. Use a geometric print or a plaid yoke with a floral print shirt in the same colors. Use contrasting solid colors for yoke and shirt. Make a matching solid-color and print combination. Contrast dazzling white collar, cuffs, and polo opening with dark solid or print for a spic-and-span summer look.

Shirts for the Sporting Life   Denim is one good choice for shirts and shirt jackets for active sports and outdoor wear. This sturdy twill-weave fabric is frequently made of cotton but also comes in synthetics. Blue is a standard favorite, but a variety of colors, including faded blue, and plaids and stripes are available. The fabric is comfortable to wear, easy to care for, and requires no special handling during construction. For the Western look use flat-felled seams. Make shirts from light, jackets from heavy denim.

Trial Fabric   If you plan to test your shirt pattern with a trial garment (see page 97), you will want to purchase fabric for your trial garment, too. Use a woven check (such as gingham) or plaid as first choice. This will enable you to see the grainline of the fabric as you are fitting the garment.

Interfacing   The shirt look may call for interfacing to give body to collar, cuffs, front opening, and buttonholes. To purchase the correct amount, remember that interfacings are cut from the same pattern and on the same grain as the part to be interfaced.

Usually you should choose interfacing that is lighter in weight than the garment fabric. Hold a piece of garment fabric over the interfacing to see how it will conform and if it will provide sufficient firmness. If interfacing is too stiff, it will impose itself on the outer fabric. If it is too limp, it will not provide the needed support.

Nonwoven interfacings are not as flexible as woven ones. Press-on interfacings are available in both woven and nonwoven materials. They are especially useful for areas where a fair degree of firmness is preferred. Press-on interfacings are not recommended for sheer fabrics. Smooth-finished fabrics, such as voile and organdy, often can be self-interfaced.

NOTIONS

When you purchase your pattern, fabric, and interfacing, you should purchase all necessary notions. Needless to say, you will need thread that matches your fabric, but you may also want thread in a contrasting color for decorative stitching. You should also purchase buttons or gripper snaps for closures and any desired trimmings. Read the sections on trims in Customizing before going shopping.

If you want to make a master pattern for the shirt look, you will need heavy nonwoven interfacing fabric, iron-on nonwoven interfacing, a product for tracing patterns, or brown paper.

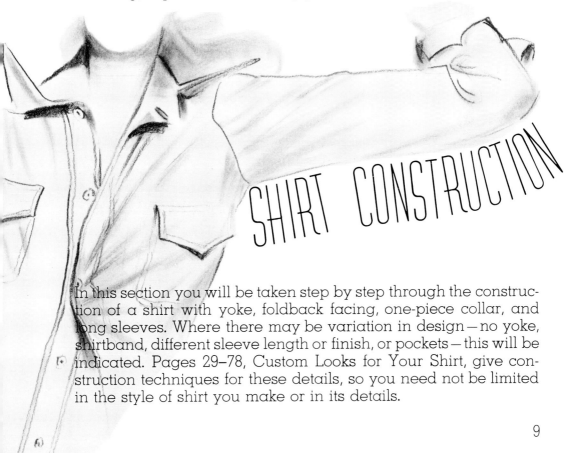

SHIRT CONSTRUCTION

In this section you will be taken step by step through the construction of a shirt with yoke, foldback facing, one-piece collar, and long sleeves. Where there may be variation in design — no yoke, shirtband, different sleeve length or finish, or pockets — this will be indicated. Pages 29–78, Custom Looks for Your Shirt, give construction techniques for these details, so you need not be limited in the style of shirt you make or in its details.

PREPARATION/CUTTING/MARKING

See It's Elementary, pages 80–86, for information on grainline, preshrinking, cutting and marking, and stitching. There are also charts for stitching and pressing special fabrics in that section. For pattern adjustment instructions see Finding the Perfect Fit, beginning on page 97.

After determining the fit of your basic pattern and before cutting your fashion fabric, read the customizing section, and select any design variations you wish to incorporate in your shirt. For a trial shirt, machine baste all seams, following the instructions for making the garment.

SHIRT BACK UNIT

YOKE
If you have a lightweight fabric, make yoke facing from same fabric as shirt. Use a lightweight yoke facing for a shirt made from medium to heavyweight fabric. Staystitch, separately, yoke and yoke facing at neckline and shoulders just outside seamline in seam allowance, in directions shown.

PLEATED BACK
Staystitch armholes and lower edge of back. Pleats give a better line to the shirt back when they are placed near the armhole edge. If you use pleats, staystitch them in position, toward side seams, stitching in the seam allowance just outside the seamline. Then, with the right sides together and shirt on top, stitch shirt back to yoke. See illustrations.

GATHERED BACK
Staystitch armhole and lower edge of back. In soft or very light-weight fabrics gathers may be preferable to pleats. Place them near armhole edges. Stitch gathers as follows: Begin at armhole seamline of shirt back, and staystitch across top edge of back a thread inside seamline, changing to longest machine stitch between each of the two sets of notches. To join gathered back to yoke, on each side of back clip long stitch nearest notch to the right, and draw up fabric until back fits yoke. Be sure sides are

10

gathered equally and that gathers are equally distributed in each side. If necessary, wind threads around pins to hold gathers before stitching. With right sides together and shirt side up, stitch back to yoke on seamline as for pleated yoke, preceding. When stitching across gathers, unwind threads from pin, and hold them firmly so they cannot slip.

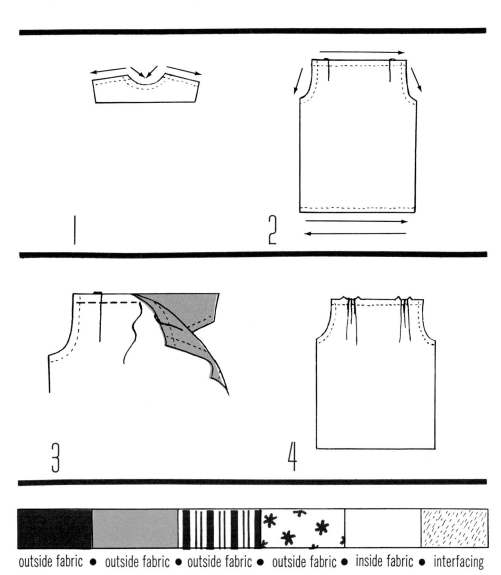

outside fabric • outside fabric • outside fabric • outside fabric • inside fabric • interfacing

JOIN YOKE FACING TO BACK

With right side of yoke facing to inside of shirt and yoke side up, stitch facing to back through stitching on seamline. Press yoke and facing seam allowance up, and trim to ¼ inch (6mm). If you like, topstitch on yoke close to seam through all thicknesses.

BACK WITHOUT YOKE

Staystitch neckline, shoulders, and armholes of shirt back. Stitch directionally, as for yoke.

SHIRT FRONT UNITS

This construction is for a foldback front facing. If you choose to make a shirtband, see instructions pages 66–67. If your fabric pins well, mark facing foldline as follows. Clip into front facing foldline at top and bottom ⅛ inch (3mm). Mark top layer on wrong side with tracing paper and wheel. Place three or four pins with small heads through both layers of fabric on the marking line. Turn top facing back along pins, and press on foldline (line of pins). Remove pins. Turn the two front pieces so the side that was pressed is underneath. Fold upper shirt front facing back along foldline of under shirt front. Press second facing in position.

To mark a fabric that will not hold pins or handle well for the preceding method, mark both layers on wrong side of fabric at foldline with tracing paper and wheel. Use a running hand stitch to trace foldline so it can be seen on right side of fabric. Press each facing in place from right side.

Staystitch neckline, shoulders, and armholes just outside seamline in seam allowance, in directions shown. Staystitch facing and hem edge of shirt ¼ inch (6mm) from edges. (If facing edge **a** is a selvage it will not require staystitching.) Use machine or hand basting to mark center front lines and positions of buttonholes and pockets. If your pattern has darts, stitch them. Press over a cushion, shaping carefully. Horizontal darts are pressed down; vertical darts are pressed toward center front or back.

Depending on your fabric and preference, you may use regular interfacing, either woven or nonwoven, or you may use the iron-on variety. If you plan to use iron-on interfacing, press a small

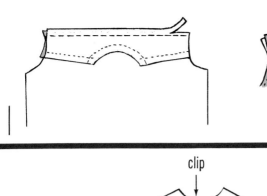

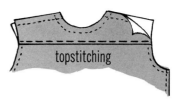
topstitching

1

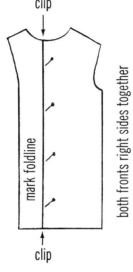

clip

mark foldline

both fronts right sides together

clip

2

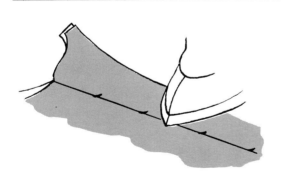

3

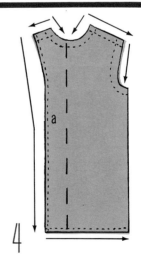

a

4

piece to a scrap of your fabric to be sure that it will adhere well. Cut two iron-on interfacings the size of the facings; trim away ¼ inch (6mm) at outer edges **a** and **b** as shown. Trim to foldline of hem at lower edges, and trim to seam allowances at neckline Press to wrong sides of facings.

If you are using woven interfacing, tear or cut it on grain. Cut nonwoven interfacing, which has no grain direction. Make two strips 1½ to 2 inches (3.8 to 5cm) wide. These will reinforce the shirt fronts for buttons and buttonholes. The strips can extend to tops of facings or the tops of highest button and buttonhole and 1 inch (2.5cm) below lowest button and buttonhole. Place strips on facings ⅛ inch (3mm) from foldline, and stitch them in place at edges **a, b, c,** and **d.** If interfacing is nonwoven, or if edge **f** is cut on selvage, it will not need to be stitched to facing. After applying interfacing, clean finish facing edges **f** and **e.** Staystitch ¼ inch (6mm) from raw edge, turn raw edge under on staystitching line, and topstitch close to folded edge.

SHIRT WITH YOKE
Here is a professional way to stitch shirt front to yokes. The front is stitched between yoke and yoke facing in one operation. Lay shirt down right side out, fronts on top. Place right upper shirt front between yoke and yoke facing, as at **a.** This is the way it will lie when finished. All the seam allowances are turned up inside the yokes. Reach between the yoke and yoke facing from the armhole side, and pull the seam allowances through to the outside. (The neck edges of shirt and yokes can be pulled through far enough to give room for stitching.) Match three seamlines; pin; stitch.

Trim seam to ¼ inch (6mm); turn, and press. Repeat for other front yoke seam. If you like, topstitch yoke through all thicknesses. Staystitch armhole edges of yoke together from front to back.

SHIRT WITHOUT YOKE
Join shirt fronts to shirt backs at shoulder seams, stitching from neckline to armhole on each side.

If you have not already made a master pattern, you may wish to baste in one sleeve and baste the side seams of shirt and underarm sleeve seam for fitting shirt. Remove basting after fitting.

14

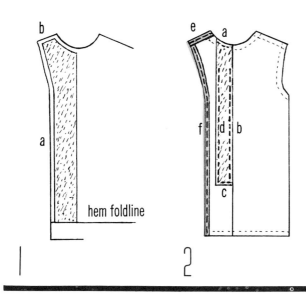

b

a

hem foldline

1

e a

f d b

c

2

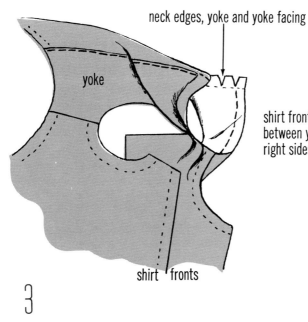

neck edges, yoke and yoke facing

yoke

shirt front, right side up, lies
between yoke and yoke facing,
right sides together

shirt   fronts

3

COLLAR UNIT

Construction of two other collars is given, pages 30–35. A method for making a one-piece collar is given here.

The collar pattern should be cut twice—for the upper and under collars. In heavy fabrics to allow for turn-of-cloth (the slightly larger size of the top collar necessary for it to lie flat) trim ⅛ inch (3mm) from under collar along outside edge.

Cut interfacing same size as under collar. If you are using iron-on interfacing (**a**), cut ½ inch (1.3cm) from all edges. Apply with heat to inside of under collar according to manufacturer's instructions. If you are using stitched-on interfacing (**b**), trim corners diagonally ¼ inch (6mm) from each edge. Stitch to inside of under collar on seamline except at neck edge; stitch here just outside seamline in seam allowance. Stitch in correct direction of grain. Trim interfacing to seamline.

With right sides of collar together, stitch ends and outside edges in direction shown. Press seam open on edge presser. Trim seam allowance to ¼ inch (6mm). Turn collar. To turn the corner perfectly, use a needle and thread to take a very small stitch across the corner through the seamline. Drop needle, and lift (do not pull) on threads. Remove threads after perfecting corner. Press collar, pinning it over cushion and molding it carefully, using steam if your fabric permits. Allow collar to dry on cushion before removing.

ATTACH COLLAR

If you are making the one-piece collar described in the preceding section use the instructions given here for attaching to shirt. Methods for attaching one-piece collar with neckband and collar with separate neckband are given with instructions for those collars, pages 30–34.

Clip neck edge of shirt at intervals almost to staystitching to straighten curve for stitching. Key and pin center back of under collar to center back of shirt and ends of collar to center fronts of shirt. With shirt side up, stitch under collar to shirt between notches (between shoulder seams for a no-yoke shirt), to approximately one inch from each end of collar. Key raw edges of top

16

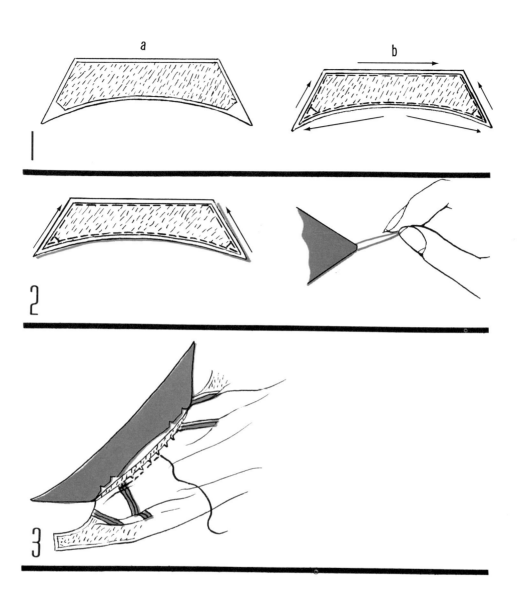

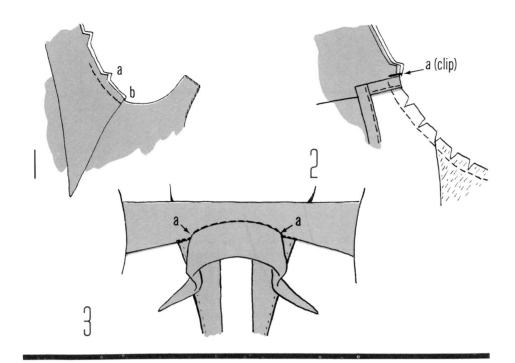

collar and under collar; stitch to shirt near seamline in seam allowance from each end of collar to yoke or shoulder seam.

Clip facings almost to staystitching at intervals to straighten curve for stitching. With shirt right side out and collar in place at neckline, fold back front facings over top collar, right sides of facings to right side of shirt. Pin in position. With shirt-side up, stitch on seamline through all thicknesses from edge of facing to shoulder or yoke seam on each side. Trim all of the collar seams to ¼ inch (6mm), and clip curves where necessary. Clip into under collar seam at edge of facings, **a.** Across back of shirt turn under collar seam up into collar, and press.

Clip to seamline on top collar at ends of front facings, **a.** Turn top collar under on seamline; topstitch on seamline of under collar, or on soft fabrics slipstitch to undercollar on seamline. Hand stitch edges of facings to shirt, or machine stitch from right side of shirt through wells of yoke or shoulder seams. Press collar and neckline edge over press cushion. A back neck facing is not desirable with this type of collar.

18

SHIRT SLEEVES

If you intend to use plackets with the cuffs of your shirt sleeves, choose one of the three on pages 36–42 that is appropriate for your shirt and fabric. Make the placket before making the rest of the sleeve. To make a sleeveless shirt, see pages 46–48; to finish short sleeves, see pages 44–46 before proceeding.

The following technique for joining sleeves to shirt gives the flat sleevecap traditional for shirts. The sleeve hangs differently as a result of using this method. Some patterns use the traditional set-in sleeve with more fullness in the sleevecap, which gives the look of a blouse to a shirt. If your pattern requires, use the second method, Set-in Sleeves.

Clip armhole at intervals to give a straighter line for stitching. Do not clip staystitching. With right sides together pin sleeve to armhole edge. (Be sure you have correct sleeve for armhole.) With sleeve side up, sew sleeve to armhole, easing in sleeve between notches. It is easier to stitch with the outside curve (sleeve) up. Press seam toward sleeve.

4

Join side seams of shirt and sleeve, right sides together, in a continuous line of stitching from hemline of shirt to end of sleeve. Choose seam finish according to your fabric and the style of your shirt. See pages 58–63 for seams and seam finishes.

5

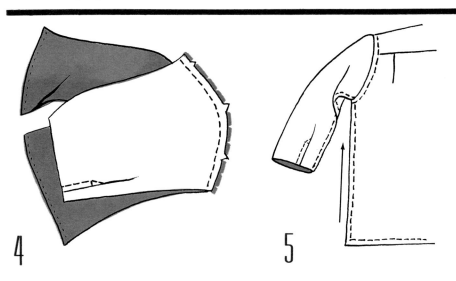

4   5

SET-IN SLEEVES

If you are making set-in sleeves, join the shirt back and fronts at the side seams before proceeding. Stitch from hemline to armhole. Press seams open. See pages 58–63 if your fabric requires a seam finish. Prepare sleevecap according to fabric — woven or knit. Both methods follow.

SLEEVECAP, WOVEN FABRICS

With matching thread and precisely on the ⅝-inch (1.5cm) seamline, staystitch cap of sleeve, changing to the longest stitch between notches. On crease-resistant fabrics and others that resist molding by pressing, use a slightly shorter stitch. (The space between stitches will be shorter, and the fabric will mold and shrink more easily. This will control the ease over the cap.) Clip bobbin thread at front and back notches, and draw up bobbin thread to ease sleevecap. This is known as the ease-line method.

SLEEVECAP, KNIT FABRICS

If you are working with a knit fabric, staystitch around entire sleevecap ½ inch (1.3cm) from the edge. Then place a row of baste stitching from notch to notch within the seam allowance, ¼ inch (6mm) from the first line. To prepare sleeve to set in armhole, draw up baste stitching only. The knit will mold beautifully at the staystitching line without being drawn up there.

COMPLETE SLEEVE

Stitch and press sleeve darts, if any. Match side of sleeve at seamline. Pin, and stitch from armhole down. Ease back to front over elbow if pattern requires. Note that some finishes require sleeve seams to be stitched during or after completion of sleeve finish (cuff and placket, if any). Complete sleeve and sleeve finish in order required for the sleeve you are making.

SETTING IN SLEEVE

Check sleeves and notches to be sure you match sleeves to the correct armholes. Lay garment and sleeve right sides out. Insert your hand first through sleeve, then through armhole, and turn garment back over sleeve. Right sides will be together. Pin notch at top of sleeve to match shoulderline. Key and pin underarm of

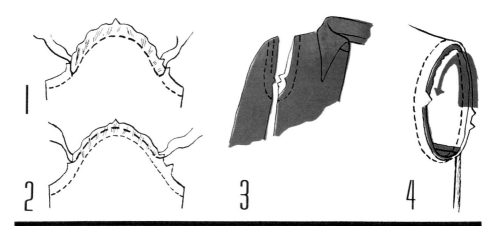

sleeve and garment. If the hang of sleeves was corrected during fitting and new keying points marked, be sure to key and pin at the new markings.

Adjust ease to fit armhole by drawing up bobbin thread again, as needed. Do not pull too tightly. Do not stretch armhole to fit sleeve. Distribute ease. There must not be so much that little pleats or gathers form anywhere in the sleevecap. Remove sleeve from armhole. Shrink out ease of sleevecap on end of cushion. Steam press with point of iron at seamline to form a smooth, round cap. There can be little pleats in the seam allowance but never at the line of stitching.

Replace sleeve in garment, right sides together, and pin. To sew in sleeve, begin stitching at underarm with sleeve on top. Stitch all the way around the circle, one thread inside the ease stitching. The underarm seam can be reinforced by stitching the underarm again between the two notches. To reduce bulk with heavy fabrics, you can trim underarm seam to ¼ inch (6mm). On knits, trim entire armhole seam to ¼ inch (6mm).

Final press armhole seam only across the top between notches. With sleeve turned into garment, extend upper seam allowances outward. Press them together on a cushion or the edge of a sleeveboard with point of iron toward seamline. When pressed in this way, the seam allowances can be turned to lie in the sleeve. This will give the sleevecap a rounded, rolled look. Do not press seam allowance into sleeve.

CUFFS

Make the cuff for a long sleeve after the placket has been made and the underarm sleeve has been sewn. If this is a shirt-style sleeve, this will mean that the sleeve and body of the shirt have been joined.

Cuffs are cut lengthwise and, unless they are shaped, the outside edges are cut on a fold. Interfacings are cut on the same grain unless they are nonwoven; they may be cut on the bias if the style or fabric requires some resilience. A method for making a closed cuff without placket is given pages 41–42. Cuffs for short sleeves are given on pages 44–46.

Cut interfacing for under cuff to extend ¼ inch (6mm) beyond foldline. Stitch interfacing to inside of under cuff ½ inch (1.3cm) — ¾ inch (3cm) for heavy fabrics — from side edges, ¼ inch (6mm) from raw crosswise edge and ¼ inch (6mm) from fold. Trim interfacing for heavy fabrics to stitching except at foldline. Mark buttonholes on interfacing, and baste to mark right side.

Pleats or gathers are used to fit the sleeve to the cuff. If sleeve will be gathered into cuff, make a row of long stitches at sleeve edge. Leave ends unknotted. Lay right side of under cuff on wrong side of sleeve. Pin in position at seamline. If pleats are to be used, place them on either side of placket, turned toward opening. For gathers pull up gathering stitches to fit sleeve to cuff. Gathers should be evenly distributed. Stitch cuff to sleeve on seamline with sleeve side up.

Turn ends of cuff right sides together. Stitch one end of cuff on seamline, beginning at lower edge. Continue to sew on seamline across top of cuff, through seam joining under cuff to sleeve, for 1 inch (2.5cm). Tuck sleeve in to keep out of way when stitching. Repeat stitching at other end of cuff and across top for 1 inch (2.5cm). Trim sleeve and cuff seam allowances to ¼ inch (6mm). Round off seam allowance at corners to reduce bulk.

Turn cuff right side out. Turn in seam allowance at opening, and topstitch across this edge of cuff, close to edge, from one side of placket opening to the other. On soft fabrics, a second row of stitching ½ inch (1.3cm) below top of cuff is desirable. Make buttonholes, and sew on buttons.

22

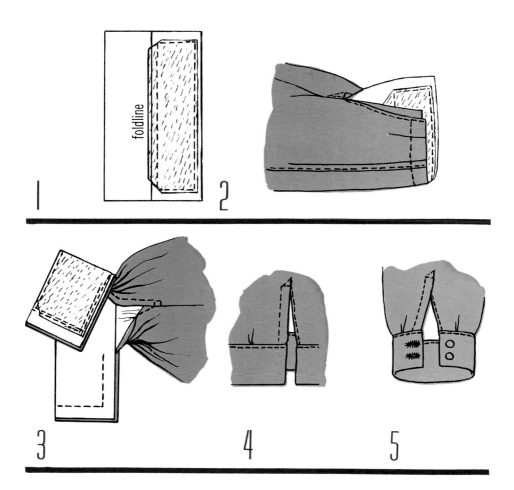

HEM

The hem you choose for your shirt will depend upon how you intend to wear it (outside or tucked in), the fabric from which it is made, and the shirt style. See pages 62–64 to choose hem and to find instructions for hemming.

TOPSTITCHING

Where topstitched details are used for a decorative or well-tailored look, be sure your stitching is completely accurate. A line of machine basting will serve as a guide. You can also use your seam guide or an adhesive tape made for this purpose that can

23

be detached from fabric easily after stitching is completed. Use a regulation stitch through all thicknesses. Stitch slowly but steadily. See page 77 for variations in topstitching.

Fronts may be topstitched to correspond with topstitching on the collar. On a one-piece collar the topstitching should sink into the well of the seamline (**a**). At top of shirt front the topstitching should make the same angle at **b** as it does at the point of the collar. See the illustration. Do not lockstitch, but leave long threads at either end of stitching. Draw threads to underside and knot them.

staystitching • staystitching • staystitching •   stitching • stitching • stitching

FRONT CLOSURES

GRIPPER SNAPS
Gripper fasteners used instead of buttonholes and buttons give a shirt a sporty look. They are very easy to apply.

BUTTONHOLES
Vertical buttonholes are used for men's shirts. Women should follow their preference for either vertical or horizontal buttonholes. Many shirt looks for women, even in dresses, currently use vertical buttonholes, but horizontal buttonholes give more secure closure at the bustline for women with large busts. Women's shirts button right over left; men's, left over right. Consider making buttons and buttonholes in groupings of two or three for design interest. Several buttons and buttonholes are fashionable on cuffs. Match the groupings on the shirt front and cuffs.

Buttonhole placement should be checked during fitting. Figures with large busts always require a buttonhole and button at the level of the apex, or crown, of the bust. Buttonholes should be evenly spaced. The pattern placement should be correct unless the length has required alteration. In this case, repositioning will be necessary. Retain top buttonhole placement; then position bustline buttonhole before spacing the rest of buttonholes. Do not make a buttonhole at the neckband if your shirt is made from bulky or slippery fabric on which it will be difficult to make a neat buttonhole. (Buttonholes are difficult to make in this area, in any case, because of the small area and the kind of construction involved in making them.)

Vertical buttonholes should be made on the center front line. Crosswise buttonholes should extend ⅛ inch (3mm) from the center front line toward the edge. This permits the buttons, when buttoned, to lie exactly on the center line. Make buttonholes ⅝ inch (1.5cm) long for ½-inch (1.3-cm) shirt buttons. The final positions should be marked with basting. If your sewing machine makes buttonholes, follow instructions given in your manual. If you are using a commercial attachment, follow instructions that accompany it to make your buttonholes.

25

BUTTONS

A row of topstitching on the center front gives a line for sewing on buttons and, in softer fabrics, helps hold the facing in place. Except on a print where it will not show, end stitching at level of top button. Buttons are sewed to the shirt after all other construction has been completed. To mark positions of buttons, lay the shirt so the two front edges align exactly, facings back to back, right sides of shirt to outside. Use pins to hold in place. Place a pin through the front of each buttonhole at the center front line. This marks the correct place to attach button.

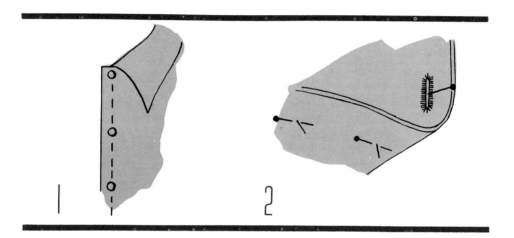

Reinforce buttons on heavy fabric with a small stay button on inside of garment. As you attach outer button, sew through the stay button, too. Use a double strand of thread with a secure knot at each end. Knotting the ends separately keeps them from twisting. Conceal thread knots as you begin. Slip needle under button and through fabric, using a small stitch to secure thread and knot in

outside fabric ● outside fabric ● outside fabric ● outside fabric ● inside fabric ● interfacing

fabric. To obtain a thread shank, lay a bobby pin over the button between the holes, and stitch over it. Remove the bobby pin when you have made enough stitches through button to hold it securely. Secure thread under button with several back stitches. The extra thread used to stitch around the bobby pin provides a thread shank for ease when garment is buttoned.

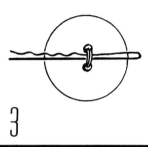

3

FINAL PRESSING

Remove any baste stitches that remain. Brush lint and stray threads from the garment. Examine the fabric for iron shine, iron marks, wrinkles, and areas that need special attention. Touch up all key points — neck and armhole edges, facings, and hems. Always follow correct grain direction. If necessary, go over darts and seams again from the wrong side. Press lightly to prevent edges from leaving an impression on the outside of the garment, or use paper or cardboard strips under seam allowances and construction details.

Use cushion, paper strips, or pounding block where they were used in construction pressing. (See tables pages 92–95.) Final pressing is done on the right side of the garment unless the fabric absolutely prevents this. Be sure to use an appropriate press cloth. Brown paper or tissue paper (if the iron is not too hot) make good press cloths here, as they leave no troublesome lint on your fabric. The collar should be molded and shaped over a cushion. Use the iron carefully on the lengthwise grain, including hem.

CUSTOM LOOKS FOR YOUR SHIRT

When you have made some basic decisions about your pattern—whether you will want a yoke (don't use one if you have shoulder fitting problems), whether you need bust darts or not (women with large bust sizes should use them), whether you will want a one-piece or a two-piece collar—you will be able to think in terms of variations you can use to make your shirt truly yours. With the use of the variations in this section you can make a closetful of shirts, each customized for you.

The same shirt pattern can be used for a variety of looks by the use of different fabrics—anything from denim to satin, with appropriate buttons and trims. Make a shirt, shirt jacket, shirt dress, or floor-length dress. Consider using a tunnel waist or a self-belt with a shirt jacket or dress. Vary the sleeve length for different looks. Use different kinds of cuffs. Change the number and/or placement of pockets. Put one on a sleeve, use two on a side, vary the shapes. Add curved or straight side vents to a shirt.

Round the collar points for a demure look in dotted Swiss or dainty floral print. Use one of the methods on pages 66–69 for making a shirtband or polo opening.

Add any of the suggested trims on pages 76–78 to suit your fabric and taste, or make a harmonizing ascot. The possibilities are endless. Create a wardrobe of shirt looks that has your individual stamp. This section tells you how.

COLLAR WITH SEPARATE NECKBAND

Cut interfacing on the same grain as collar (except nonwoven interfacing, which has no grain direction). Iron-on interfacing will give some additional firmness, an advantage for this collar. Interfacing is applied to the under collar except for voile, silk, and other lightweight fabrics, where applying interfacing to the top collar will cushion seams and give the collar a smoother finish.

If you are using iron-on interfacing, trim ½ inch (1.3cm) from edges and trim corners diagonally ¼ inch (6mm) from each side of corner, as shown. Apply using manufacturer's instructions.

Trim corners of regular interfacing as for iron-on interfacing, in preceding paragraph. Stitch to under or top collar, depending on fabric, on seamline except at lower edge. At lower edge staystitch under collar just outside seamline in seam allowance. Trim interfacing to stitching.

An extra piece of interfacing may be used to give additional firmness to collar points. Place the pieces to extend 2 or more inches (5 or more cm) from points, as shown. Pin to first layer of interfacing. Stitch or fuse in position.

Collars in heavy or bulky fabrics can be made and turned more easily if points are rounded off.

30

To stitch a seam with a sharp angle, use reinforcement (short) stitches on each side of the angle. To change directions for angle pivot with needle in fabric, take one or two short stitches across corner, pivot fabric again, and continue stitching. Change to regulation stitching a short distance beyond the corner.

Stitch collar to under collar at ends and outside edge, with right sides together and under collar on top. (If you stitched interfacing to collar, sew through the first line of stitches.) Press seams open

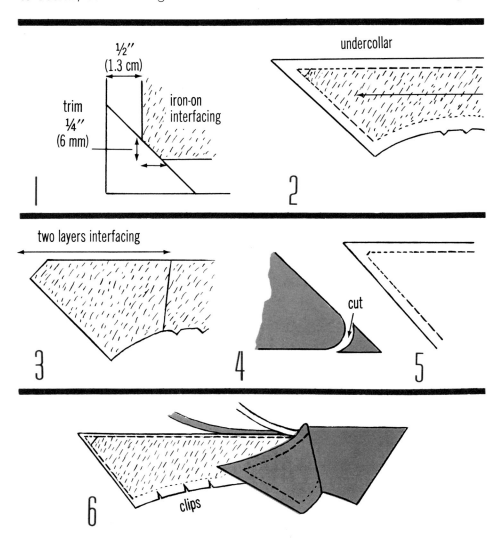

31

on edge presser, trim to scant ¼ inch (6mm), and clip where necessary for collar to lie flat. Turn collar right side out. Use thread and needle to stitch into seam from outside at point. Lift gently on thread to pull corner to right side. Press. Stitch together, just outside seamline in seam allowance, the edges (**a**) of collar. Topstitch outer edges of collar if you wish.

2. Apply interfacing to the inside of one neckband in the same way you applied interfacing to collar. Trim ½ inch (1.3cm) off all edges of iron-on interfacing, and apply according to manufacturer's directions. Stitch other interfacing to neckband on seamline.

3. The collar will be stronger if the interfaced neckband is attached to the under collar side. Stitch the under collar to interfaced neckband, right sides together, with the neckband on top. Trim stitched-on interfacing to seamlines.

4. Staystitch the neck edge of top (non-interfaced) neckband just outside the seamline in the seam allowance. Lay this neckband on the top collar, right sides together, with neckband on top, and, with the interfaced neckband turned back below under collar, stitch

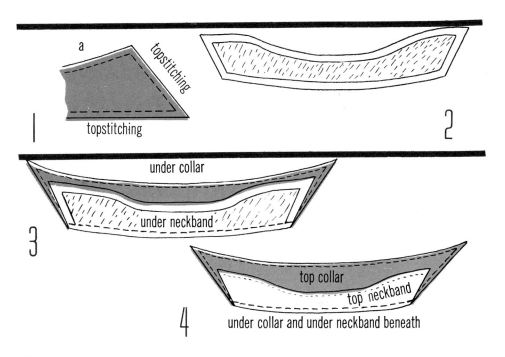

a

topstitching

topstitching

1

2

under collar

under neckband

3

top collar

top neckband

under collar and under neckband beneath

4

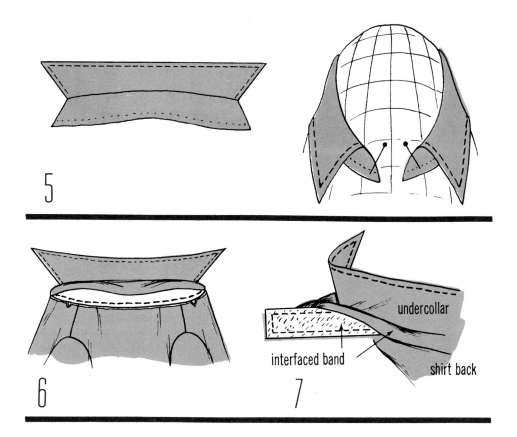

non-interfaced neckband to top collar on seamline. Press seam open, and trim to scant ¼ (6mm). Turn bands down, and press. Pin and mold collar on press cushion. Allow to dry completely before removing from cushion.

The front facings or shirtbands should be completed and stitched in place on shirt fronts before collar is attached to shirt. Place top (non-interfaced) band with its right side to wrong side of shirt, neck edges together. Stitch on seamline, shirt side up.

The following is an especially fine method for completing the ends of the neckband. Turn both top and under neckbands toward collar. (Collars will lie between the two bands.) Fold collar point out of way, as shown. Stitch top and under band ends together along seamline, with top band uppermost. Begin and end stitching 1 inch (2.5cm) beyond end of bands. Repeat for other side of collar.

Trim all of seam allowance to scant ¼ inch (6mm). Turn neckband right side out. Press seam allowance on top band up toward neckband; trim seam allowance to ¼ inch (6mm). Edgestitch open edge of interfaced band to outside of shirt. Continue edgestitching all around neckband. Press. Continue with shirt construction.

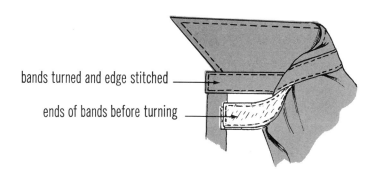

bands turned and edge stitched

ends of bands before turning

COLLAR AND NECKBAND CUT IN ONE

This collar is somewhat simpler to make than the preceding collar, but it cannot fit around the neckline as well. However, the fit is acceptable when the collar is made in a soft fabric, or if it is to be worn wide open at the neckline.

The collar pattern should be cut twice—for upper and under collars. In heavy fabrics to allow for turn-of-cloth (the slightly larger size of the top collar necessary for it to lie flat), trim ⅛ inch (3mm) from under collar on edges **a, b,** and **c.**

Cut interfacing from collar pattern. If you are using iron-on interfacing, cut ½ inch (1.3cm) from all edges. Apply with heat to inside of under collar according to manufacturer's instructions. If you are using stitched-on interfacing, trim corners diagonally ¼ inch (6mm) from each edge. See illustration, page 31. Stitch to inside of under collar on seamline except at neck edge; stitch here just outside seamline in seam allowance. Stitch in correct direction of grain. Trim interfacing to seamline.

34

Stitch under collar between notches of neck edge in a continuous line, one row across foldline and three rows beneath it, each row ¼ inch (6mm) from the one above, as shown.

For soft knits and fabrics of similar texture, one row of stitching all the way across the foldline will serve to shape the collar. Do this stitching after top and under collar have been joined.

Staystitch neck edge of top collar just outside seamline. With right sides of top and under collar together and under collar toward you, stitch two collars together. Press as much of seam as possible open on edge presser. Clip to seamline on sides **a** and **b,** as shown. Trim seams; turn collar, and press it, molding over a cushion. Allow to dry on cushion before proceeding with construction.

Stitch through top and under collar on foldline if fabric is soft or a knit. Do not topstitch this collar until it has been applied to shirt. Use the same method for attaching as for the Collar with Separate Band, preceding.

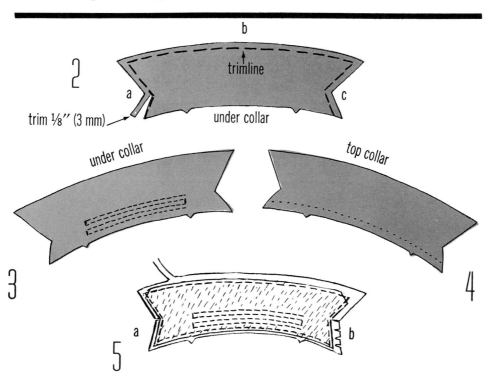

b

trimline

a

c

trim ⅛″ (3 mm)

under collar

under collar

top collar

a

b

CUFFS AND PLACKETS

BOUND PLACKET

This placket is also known as a continuous, or lap, placket. Stitch around placket as marked on pattern. Use reinforcement stitching for about ½ inch (1.3cm) on each side of point **a,** and take one stitch straight across the point. Slash on pattern line.

Cut a strip on lengthwise grain 1½ inches (3.8cm) wide and twice the length of the opening. Staystitch strip ¼ inch (6mm) from edge. This staystitching serves as a bridge on which to turn hem edge. Turn one edge to inside along staystitch line, and press.

Lay sleeve wrong side up, spread slash open, and place strip right side down on sleeve, unpressed edge along slash line as shown. Turn sleeve side up, and stitch along staystitching. At the point **a** leave needle in fabric, lift presser foot, and adjust sleeve and strip to stitch second half. On the underside press strip and seam allowance away from sleeve. Turn pressed hem edge of strip over seam allowance, and topstitch in position at machine, or slipstitch by hand. Press the placket in place, lapping the back edge under the front. To keep placket in position, turn sleeve to wrong side and stitch across placket at angle as shown, or top-stitch it in position from the right side.

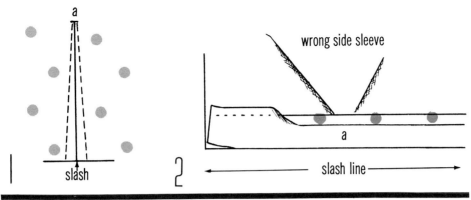

a

slash

1

2

wrong side sleeve

a

slash line

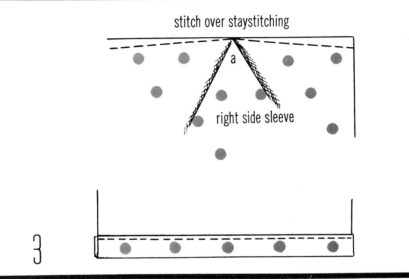

stitch over staystitching

a

right side sleeve

3

4

PLACKET WITH HEM

This is a very simple, strong, and effective placket made with either machine or hand stitching. Slash fabric on marked pattern line. (Always slash on straight of grain.) Clip crosswise at end of slash ⅛ inch (3mm) on each side. If fabric requires, staystitch slash ⅛ inch (3mm) from edges. Turn underlap edge (narrow side of sleeve) to wrong side ⅛ inch (3mm) on staystitching line; press; turn under again ⅛ inch (3mm). Press, and stitch a ⅛-inch (3-mm) hem at machine, or slipstitch by hand.

Turn overlap side of placket (wide side of sleeve) edge under ⅛ inch (3mm), and press. Turn under a second time ¼ to ½ inch (6mm to 1.3cm), depending on how easily the fabric can be turned, and stitch hem in position by machine or hand. Lap top (wide side) over under placket on right side, forming pleat in sleeve above placket. Hold pleat in place with a triangle of stitching, catching raw edges on underside in the stitching.

For a French cuff, follow the same procedure, but before applying cuff turn underlap (narrow) side to inside the width of its hem.

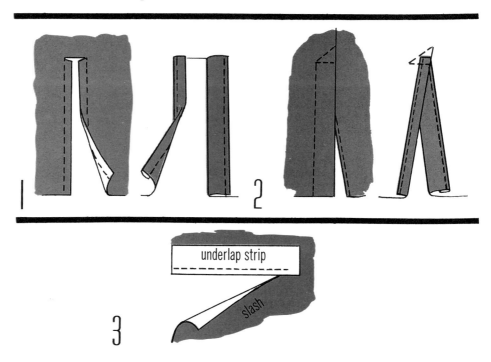

underlap strip

slash

38

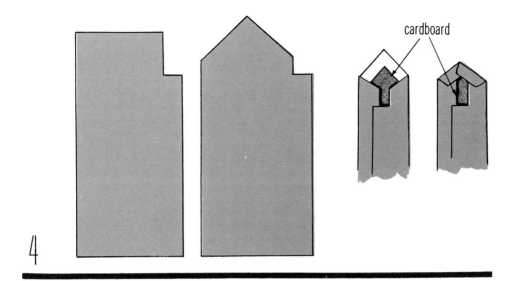

cardboard

CLASSIC PLACKET

For a shirt jacket or a finely tailored shirt or dress, a separate facing looks custom-made. Directions on pattern instruction sheets often are confusing and difficult. This technique is easy and results in a well-made placket.

Slash placket opening on grain. If fabric requires, staystitch both edges ¼ inch (6mm) from edge. To narrow side of sleeve (which will be the placket underlap) stitch a straight strip of fabric 1½ inches (3.8cm) wide and ¾ inch (2cm) longer than opening. Right sides should be together. Stitch ¼ inch (6mm) from edge along the length and ¼ inch (6mm) beyond the top of slash.

If you do not have a pattern, make an overlap strip on lengthwise grain 3 inches (7.5cm) wide and long enough to finish 1¼ inches (3.2cm) above placket opening.

Turn under seam allowance on overlap facing; press. You may wish to use a pointed placket instead of one that is square-finished. Cut end of facing according to your choice. To fold and press a pointed end, see illustration. Press over a small triangle of cardboard, as shown, to shape point. A square end also can be shaped over cardboard. Press the foldline that will be the edge of finished overlap.

Stitch overlap facing to wide side of sleeve, right side of overlap to wrong side of sleeve. Stitch ¼ inch (6mm) from edge along length and same distance beyond top of slash. Clip seam allowance diagonally to corners at top of placket, forming a triangle as shown. Press underlap seam allowance toward underlap strip. Turn ¼ inch (6mm) on unstitched edge toward side, and press. Fold underlap over seam allowance with pressed fold covering the first stitching. Press in place. On the wrong side, edgestitch underlap along first stitching line. Finish is ½ inch (1.3cm) wide.

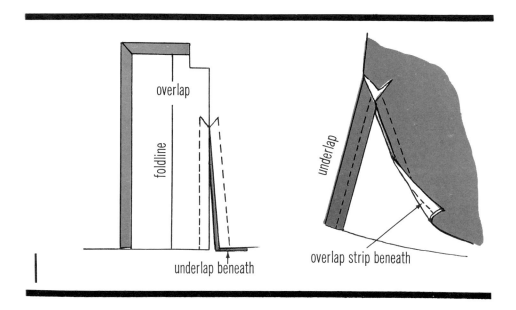

overlap

foldline

underlap beneath

underlap

overlap strip beneath

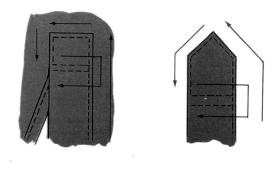

2

Press seam open on overlap, and turn the overlap to right side of sleeve. Press it in place. Beginning at sleeve edge, topstitch the side edge of overlap around square top or point, down the outside edge to the placket opening, and across the top of opening twice to strengthen it and conceal raw edges.

Some other sleeve finishes occasionally used do not make for a custom-look in a completed garment: These include the slashed opening with a fitted facing, the lapped closing with a rolled hem, and the casing with elastic. (See illustrations.)

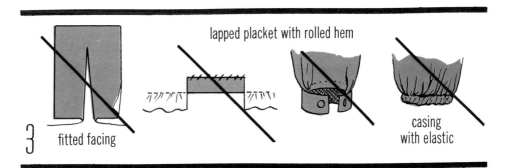

lapped placket with rolled hem

fitted facing

casing with elastic

CLOSED CUFF WITHOUT PLACKET

Stitch lower edge of sleeve with gathering stitches ⅝ inch (1.5cm) from edge. For bulky fabrics, the sleeve at lower edge before gathering should be no more than 6 inches (15cm) wider than the cuff to insure a neat finish.

Fold cuff in half lengthwise, right sides out, and press. Pin the two ends together at seamline. Check fit to see if cuff slides over hand. Fit cuff to your satisfaction. Allow for the thickness of the seam, which will take up some ease. Trim off any unnecessary amount. [Be sure to leave ⅝-inch (1.5 cm) seam allowance.]

Cut interfacing to extend ½ inch (1.3cm) beyond foldline of cuff. Stitch interfacing to under cuff ¼ inch (6mm) from the foldline. Stitch interfacing on other sides at 1 inch (2.5cm) and again at ¾ inch (2cm) from raw edges. Trim interfacing close to ¾ inch (2cm) stitching line. Trim interfacing close to ¾-inch (2-cm) stitching line. This keeps interfacing out of seamlines and eliminates bulk or wrinkles, giving a smooth finish. Do not stitch ends of cuff yet.

41

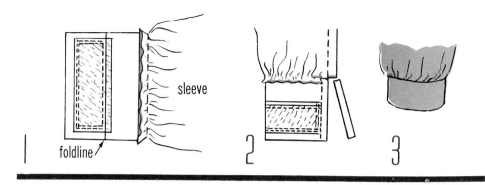

1

foldline

sleeve

2

3

Pull bobbin threads of gathering stitches at a lower sleeve edge until sleeve edge fits the cuff. For easier handling, press gathers that are inside the seamline. Pin cuff to sleeve, right sides together, the upper cuff at the sleeve edge. Stitch cuff to sleeve (sleeve on top), distributing gathers evenly and keeping them straight as you sew.

Press seam toward cuff, being careful to press only the seam, not the gathers. Trim seam to ¼ inch (6mm). With cuff extended, key and pin sleeve and cuff edges at underarm seamline, and stitch sleeve down from underarm. When you reach the under cuff, make the seamline ¾ inch (2cm) from edges to allow for turn-of-cloth when the under cuff is turned back.

Press the seam open. Trim under cuff side seam allowance to ¼ inch (6mm). Fold cuff up, and press to restore foldline crease. For bulky fabrics that will not ravel, trim under cuff to ⅛ inch (3mm) from interfacing at lower edge, and use fine stitches to whipstitch raw edges to stitching line that joined sleeve and cuff. For other fabrics, trim lower edge of under cuff to ¼ inch (6mm) from interfacing. Turn this edge under, and, with sleeve wrong side out, whipstitch to stitching line.

CUFFS: VERY SPECIAL EXTRAS

CHANGING SHAPE OF CUFF

An interesting and unusual cuff can be made by cutting diagonally lower edges **a** and **b** on top and under cuffs. Interface before

42

beginning to stitch them. The illustration shows triangles 1¼ inches (4.5cm) on a side trimmed from each corner. You can remove a smaller amount if you choose.

CHANGING POINTS TO CURVES
Curve lower edges on a cuff to eliminate making corners. You can do this on cuffs in any fabric, but you will find it easier to make cuffs from bulky fabrics—corduroy, for example—in this way. Cut corners on top and under cuffs and interfacings before beginning to stitch them.

TOPSTITCHING
On bulky fabrics it may be easier to run the topstitching off the top edges of cuffs (**c** and **d**) than to turn corners.

BUTTONHOLE STRIP
The buttonhole strip is a very nice couture touch. It also eliminates the need for making buttonholes. After making cuff and applying to shirt, sew a strip of straight or bias fabric that will have a finished width of ¼ inch (6mm) to ¾ inch (2cm) and same finished depth as cuff to the overlap edge. The width should depend on the size of the buttons. Whipstitch strip to underside of cuff. Leave openings in stitching for buttons to slip through.

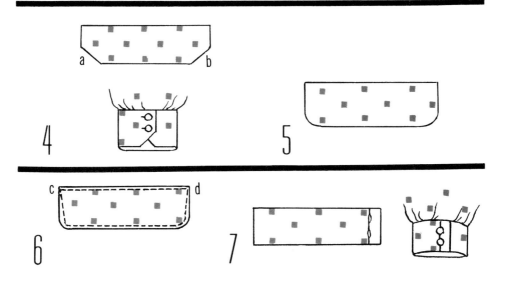

43

SHORT SLEEVE FINISHES

SIMULATED CUFF I
Before sleeve has been stitched at underarm seam, turn a hem allowance of 1¼ to 1½ inches (3.2 cm to 3.8cm) to the wrong side. (In illustration **a** is raw edge, **b** is folded edge.) Press. Turn the hem back a second time, and press lower edge. Unfold, and stitch sleeve seam in direction of grain when shirt construction requires. Press open. Restore creases at seamline.

On outside of sleeve stitch about ¼ to ⅜ inch (6mm to 1.5cm) above fold at lower edge. The raw edge is concealed in this fold and is held in place with the stitching, which forms a tuck when cuff is turned down after stitching. Press cuff in position. You may wish to add a row of topstitching the same distance from lower edge as tuck stitching is from top edge. Topstitching the hem on pocket(s) to match cuffs is a nice touch.

This is a good way to convert outgrown long sleeves on children's shirts. Press up hem and make with the sleeve seam closed.

SIMULATED CUFF II
Before sleeve seam is stitched, staystitch ¼ inch (6mm) from lower edge of sleeve. Turn hem up, and press in position. Turn raw edge of hem under on staystitching line, and press. Sew sleeve seam from armhole down. Finish as required, and press. Turn sleeve right side out. Turn hem to outside of sleeve so top of hem is at lower edge as shown. Stitch close to edge at top of hem, catching both hem and sleeve in the stitching. Turn hem down, and press.

SELF-TURNED CUFF
This cuff is much easier to press in position before sleeve seam is stitched. Finish seam allowance at lower edge of sleeve, **a,** in manner suitable for fabric. In the illustration it was clean-finished.

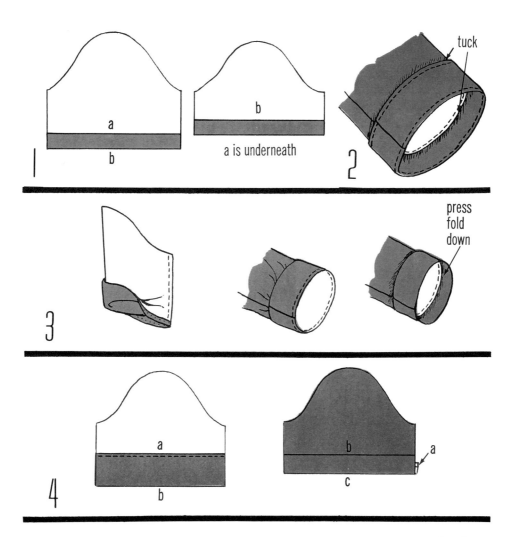

With sleeve flat, wrong side up, fold back cuff depth marked on pattern or the amount desired for depth plus about 1 inch (2.5cm) for hem allowance. Press fold at lower edge. Turn sleeve to right side; turn cuff to right side on pattern line or at depth desired. Press lower (**c**) and upper (**b**) folds carefully. Unfold cuff; stitch sleeve seam, directionally, when your shirt construction requires.

Finish seam if necessary, and press. Turn cuff to outside and into position on pressed foldlines. Press folds again, and hem inside of cuff to wrong side of garment by method appropriate for fabric.

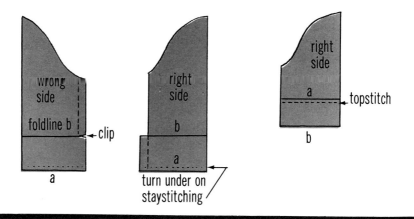

FALSE CUFF

In order to make this cuff, you must have fabric that is the same on both the right and wrong sides. Staystitch lower edge of sleeve ¼ inch (6mm) from edge. The seam must be reversed from the hem foldline to the lower edge so that the raw seams will not show when the cuff is reversed. When required in your shirt construction, stitch seam from armhole to hem foldline on wrong side as you normally would. Stop; lockstitch, and cut thread. Clip seam allowance to stitching line. Turn sleeve to right side, and complete the seam from this side. Press seams open. Turn raw edge under on staystitching. Turn, and press hem allowance to right side of sleeve. Topstitch edge of hem to sleeve to correspond with top-stitching on collar and pockets, if you like.

If you want to make a sleeveless shirt and the pattern does not include armhole facings, cut them from shirt pattern on the same grain as shirt. Make them approximately 2¾ inches (7.1cm) wide. Trim facings on seamline edges for the turn-of-the-cloth (the necessity for the outer layer of a two-layer construction to be slightly larger so it can lie flat and the under layer will not show.) Trim ⅛ inch (3mm) from the seamline edge for light to medium-weight fabrics, slightly more for heavy or bulky fabrics.

ARMHOLE FACINGS

Staystitch front and back armhole facings ½ inch (1.3cm) from inner curved edges and ¼ inch (6mm) from outer curved edges in directions shown. Stitch shoulder seams of facings, and trim to ¼ inch (6mm). Press seams open. Clean-finish outer edges, or use other finish appropriate for your fabric. (Knits do not require any further finish.) To clean-finish, turn edge under on staystitching, and stitch close to the folded edge.

Underarm seams on shirt and facing should be open when facings are applied to shirt. With garment side up and right sides together, match notches of shirt and facing, and stitch them together. Trim seam allowances to scant ¼ inch (6mm); clip curves, if necessary, so armholes will lie flat. Understitch armhole edge of facing beginning and ending 1 inch (2.5cm) from ends.

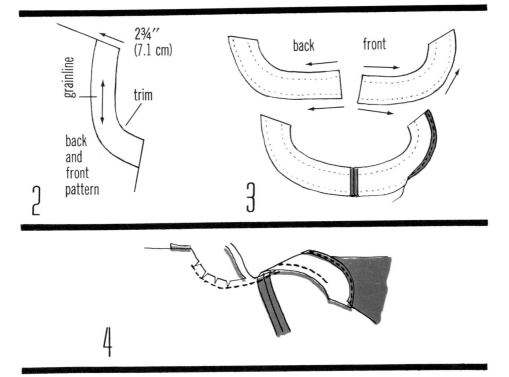

Understitching is usually placed close to the edge of a facing to catch the seam allowances of facing and garment and prevent the facing from rolling toward the outside of the garment. With garment right side out, open out facing, turn garment and facing seam allowances toward facing, and stitch them to facing close to seamline with regular machine stitches. Press on a cushion to mold facing. Work with facing to assure it will roll back into place; then top press. On fine fabrics understitch by hand.

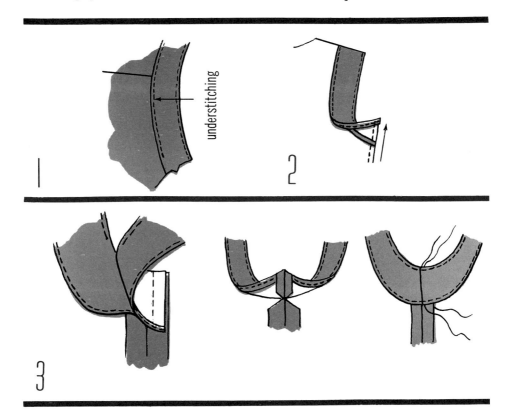

With underarm ends of facings opened out, key and pin facing and shirt underarm seam. Stitch facings and side seams directionally as shown. Finish seam as desired, and press open.

Turn facings to inside, and bar tack by hand or machine to shoulder seam. Then pin one seam of facing to corresponding seam of shirt, and stitch at machine or by hand as shown. Another technique is to catch facings to shirt at underarm by stitching at underarm, with shirt side up, through seamline for length of facing. Use machine stitching. Press underarm area.

Give a shirt your own stamp by imaginative pocket placement. For men, make the pockets with or without flaps. The number of pockets may depend on the type of shirt, and on body build. A shirt or safari jacket might use as many as four pockets—one above and one below the waistline on each side of the shirt front. Consider making pockets of contrasting fabric—for example, pockets of suede-like fabric on a sporty corduroy shirt jacket.

For women, the shapes can be as varied as your inspiration. Use flaps without pockets. Vary the shape of flaps. Placement can add individuality. Use two pockets on the same side—they can be the same or different shapes. Consider sewing a pocket on a sleeve.

Both men and women should consider placement in relation to body shape. Don't place a large or unusually shaped pocket near an area you want to minimize—large hips, for example. Try cutting pocket shapes out of paper and pinning on the shirt first to test the effect. Do not use a pocket with rounded lower edges on a plaid, striped, or checked shirt.

The pocket on a traditionally tailored shirt is placed on the left shirt front for both men and women. Even if you intend to place the pocket in this position, when trying on the shirt, pin on the pocket to see if the placement is exactly right.

ONE-LAYER PATCH POCKET

Turn under and press seam allowances on lower edge and sides.

To make a rounded pocket, staystitch on seamline; turn under seam allowance on staystitching. Clip curve so turned-back seam allowance will lie smoothly.

Fabrics that are soft, spongy, or stretchy: Press pocket seam allowances to the wrong side over a piece of cardboard the size of the finished pocket. This helps keep pocket true.

To make a pocket with corners, press folds in seam allowance at corners, as shown. To miter corners (necessary for heavy or bulky fabrics), turn seam allowance on both sides of corner to wrong side, and press in position at desired depth, using an automatic hem gauge. Fold pocket corner as shown, and press. Unfold and, with right sides together, turn creased edges down. Refold corner at angle, as shown. One angled crease should lie over the other. Stitch in the bias crease. Trim seam allowance to ⅛ inch (3mm). Press seam open on point presser. Turn edges to wrong side. Press corner.

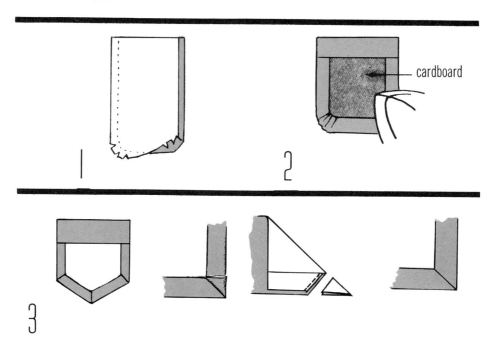

cardboard

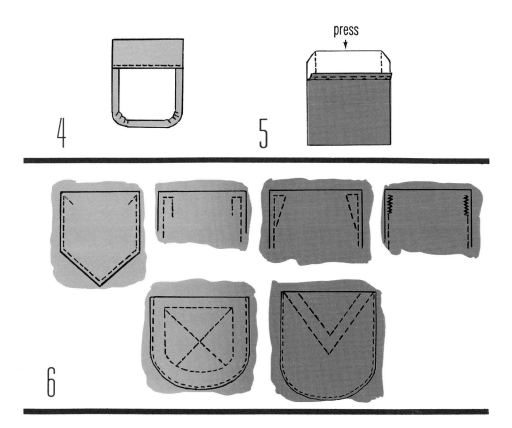

Turn back and press hem allowance at top of pocket. Staystitch
raw edge ¼ inch (6mm) from edge. For fabrics except knits (which
do not require a seam finish) turn raw edge under on staystitching; press. Stitch hem to pocket at lower edge or slipstitch.

Heavy fabrics: Staystitch top edge ¼ inch (6mm) from edge. If
desired, turn ¼ inch (6mm) under on staystitch line, and edgestitch. Press foldline; turn hem allowance to right side along this
line. Stitch to each side of pocket along seam line for depth of
hem; trim seam allowances diagonally at upper corners. Turn
hem to inside. Staystitch lower edges; Turn and finish.

To apply a one-layer patch pocket to shirt, place on marked position. Topstitch in place, close to pocket edge. For reinforcement at
upper corners end stitching as shown. If you like, vary the topstitching; see illustrations. Make up your own variation.

51

DOUBLE-LAYER PATCH POCKET

In lightweight fabrics, make the pocket from two layers of fabric. With right sides of two pockets together, stitch all around the pocket on the seamline. Trim seam to ¼ inch (6mm), trim corners diagonally to reduce bulk at seamline.

To turn to right side make a slash just long enough to turn pocket in center of under section. After pocket has been turned and pressed, the opening can be whipstitched together by hand, or it can be covered by pressing a small piece of iron-on interfacing over it. This pocket will have a perfect edge all around. Apply as for the One-Layer Patch Pocket, preceding.

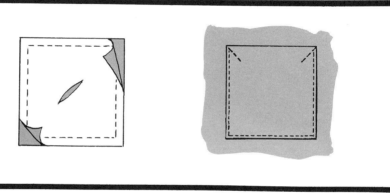

LINED PATCH POCKET

This is an outstanding technique for shirt jacket pockets in heavy fabrics. The pocket may be any shape at the lower edge. Allow 1¼ inches (3.2cm) for hem at top. The lining is cut same size as pocket, minus ¾ inch (2cm) at top. Stitch top edge of pocket to lining, right sides together, leaving ¼-inch (6-mm) seam allowance. Press seam open.

Pocket may be interfaced. Iron-on interfacing is cut the size of finished pocket. See illustration. Stitch-on interfacing is cut size of pocket to hem foldline. Stitch interfacing to pocket just outside seamline, or press in place. Trim stitched interfacing seam allowance to ¼ inch (6mm). Press top hem in place. Press under seam allowance on three sides.

Miter the corners of a square pocket in the way shown for a single-layer pocket, page 50.

To fold under the seam allowance of a rounded pocket smoothly on a curve, stitch at ¼ inch (6mm) around curved edge with a long (8 to 10) machine stitch. Leave stitching unknotted at each end. Pull up threads to shape curve carefully. Press; trim away bulk in seam allowance.

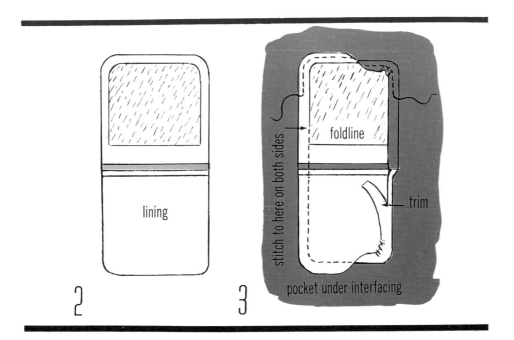

If topstitching is desired, topstitch pocket alone before applying it to garment. Place pocket on garment, and fold upper pocket out of way; only lining should be in position for stitching. Stitch lining to garment, using a seam allowance of exactly ¾ inch (2cm). Mark lining for stitching. Begin and end stitching two stitches below the hem foldline of pocket. Press seam allowance back over lining; trim. Stitch top pocket to garment by hand from the underside, using a punch stitch: Take one stitch at a time, catching underside of pocket. The needle should go straight in and straight out. The stitching should be nearly invisible from outside.

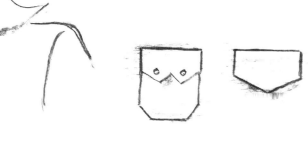

FLAP WITH OR WITHOUT POCKET

This technique eliminates raw edges at corners and a bulky seam at top of flap. The flap is cut with a fold at top. Shape of lower edge may vary. Lay pattern on fabric, folded with right sides together. To keep flap grain-perfect, cut only the top layer of fabric the shape of flap at lower edge. Leave under layer of fabric a square, larger than flap at lower edge.

If interfacing is needed, press iron-on interfacing, with seam allowances plus ⅛ inch (3mm) cut off, to wrong side of cut-out flap. Be sure fold is on grain. Stitch flap to under layer of fabric along seamlines. Press seam allowance open. Trim under layer to match cut flap, leaving ¼-inch (6-mm) seam allowance and rounding off corners.

At center top of fold, **a,** slash foldline for approximately 1½ inches (3.8cm). Turn flap through this opening. Press; topstitch sides and lower edge, if desired.

Before flap is attached, the wrong side of garment may be interfaced with a strip of fabric 1 inch (2.5cm) wide that covers the stitching line. Lay the top side of flap (the side not interfaced) to the right side of shirt, lower edge of flap toward upper edge of shirt, folded edge of flap along stitching line. Use two rows of stitches ¼ inch (6mm) apart for reinforcement. Ease flap to shirt as you stitch. Turn flap down, and press in place.

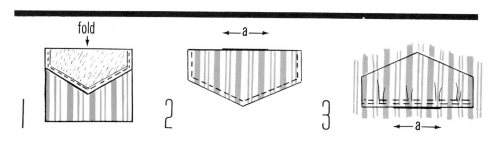

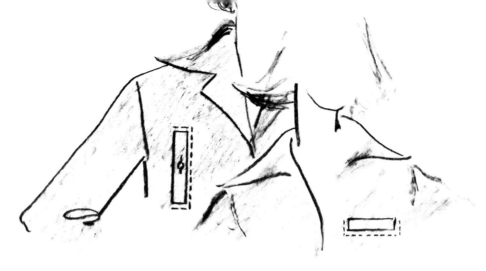

MODIFIED WELT POCKET

This is a simple, strong, and effective pocket that can be used in the chest area of shirts, jackets, and dresses made from light-weight fabric. This pocket is especially attractive when it contrasts with the garment—plain with print, crosswise with lengthwise stripes, and so on.

The location should be checked in fitting before constructing pocket. Indicate the pocket position on underside of shirt with basting thread of a contrasting color that can easily be seen on both sides of garment. The pocket should never be wider than 4 inches (10cm) or deeper than ¾ inch (2cm). Baste, still with contrasting thread, vertical lines (**c** and **c**) at each end of position to indicate ends of pocket opening. Be sure stitching is parallel and lines are of same length.

Cut a strip of fabric 1 inch (2.5cm) wider than pocket opening and twice the desired depth of pocket, plus two seam allowances. The length of the strip should be on the crosswise grain, in contrast to the grain of the garment. This piece of fabric makes the pocket welt, and upper and under pocket sections.

4

Fold pocket piece in half, right side out, and place with fold against position mark, right side of pocket to right side of garment. Unfold pocket, and with foldline still against position line, pin pocket to shirt.

On inside of garment, using presser foot as guide for straight stitching, stitch completely around position line at a distance one-half the depth desired for the finished welt [⅜ inch (1cm) if welt finishes ¾ inch (2cm) wide]. Stitch over vertical stitch marking. Make sure that both ends are stitched to exactly the same depth. Do not begin stitching at a corner. Use reinforcement stitches on each side of corners. Overlap stitching at beginning and end for security. Remove all basting stitches.

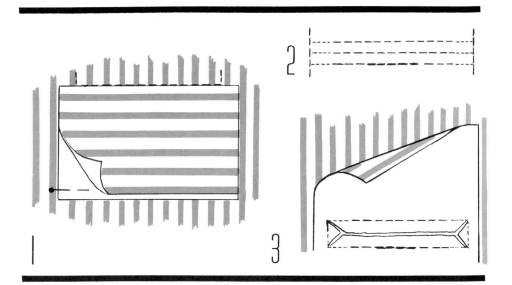

Cut between stitch lines from center toward ends, stopping ½ inch (1.3cm) from each end. Slash into corners, forming triangles at each end. Turn pocket to inside of shirt. Fold and press top of pocket piece to top seamline. Press.

Fold lower half of pocket in an even tuck, on grain, to meet upper edge of opening, **a,** and to form welt; press. On outside of shirt, stitch around ends, **c** and **c,** and lower edge, **b,** in a continuous seam, close to welt seams, as shown.

56

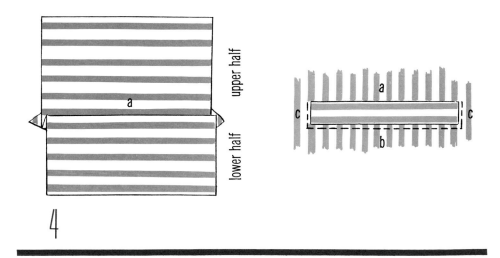

4

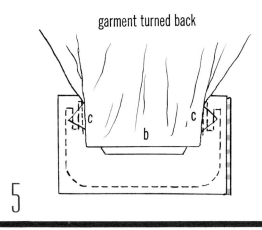

garment turned back

5

On underside fold down upper half of pocket, and key to sides of under half. With pocket side down and garment folded back on stitching at **b** and **c,** stitch back and forth across small triangle and pleat at end of opening; continue stitching around pocket, closing sides and end and rounding corners to keep out lint. Stitch twice across triangle and pleat at other side. Trim seam allowance to ¼ inch (6mm) from seam. Press pocket in position, using press cloth and/or brown paper to avoid marking top of garment with line of pocket. Press in direction of lengthwise grain.

SEAMS SEAMS SEAMS SEAMS SEAMS SEAMS SEAMS SEAMS SEAMS

The seam finish you use will depend upon the fabric and the style of your shirt. Many fabrics do not ravel in laundering or cleaning so they do not require any, but you may wish to use a seam finish just to give a finished, neat appearance inside a shirt or jacket.

PLAIN SEAM

The plain seam is simply stitched and pressed open. It is used on fabrics that do not ravel.

PINKED SEAM

For the most commonly used finish, use pinking shears to trim the edge of the seam allowance after the seam has been permanently stitched but before you press it open. Pink close to the edge so the width of the seam allowance is maintained.

EDGESTITCHED AND PINKED SEAM

Stitching and pinking a seam allowance is often used when finishing with pinking will not prevent raveling. Each seam allowance is stitched ⅛ to ¼ inch (3 to 6mm) from the edge. If the seam allowances can be pressed to lie together, they may be stitched together. Pink after stitching.

ZIGZAG FINISH

Finish each seam allowance edge with a medium-width zigzag stitch. On shirts the seams may be trimmed to ¼ inch (6mm) before zigzag stitching. Where seam allowances can be pressed to lie together, they may be stitched together.

FLAT-FELLED SEAM

A flat-felled seam gives shirts a well-tailored look. With wrong sides together, stitch a regulation ⅝-inch (1.5-cm) seam. Press the seam with both seam allowances turned in the same direction. Press across the seam to keep the fabric flat and to avoid pressing a pleat in the underside. Trim the under seam allowance to ⅛ inch (3mm); staystitch the top seam allowance ¼ inch (6mm) from seamline (width of left side of presser foot). Trim seam allowance to ⅛ inch (3mm) from staystitching line. Clip to staystitching line where necessary on curves; turn under raw edge on stay-stitching, place flat, and topstitch close to folded edge. On a well-

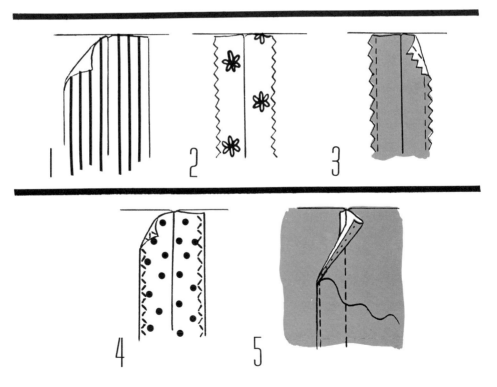

made garment, a flat-felled seam is always finished from the outside of garment to insure that the seam is smooth and straight.

MOCK FLAT-FELLED SEAM
The mock flat-felled seam is only for fabrics that do not ravel. Stitch a plain seam on the wrong side, and press both seam allowances to one side. Trim under seam allowance to ⅛ inch (3mm). Topstitch ⅜ inch (1cm) from edge of seam allowance, stitching through untrimmed seam allowance. You may wish to trim this seam after topstitching.

BOUND SEAM
The bound seam is recommended for heavy fabrics that ravel easily. Stitch, and press the seam allowances open. Encase each edge with rayon bias seam binding. Fold the binding slightly off-center, press for easier handling, and with the narrow side of the binding on top of seam allowance, stitch on edge of tape, in correct direction of grain if possible.

FRENCH SEAM
A French seam is used with lightweight and transparent fabrics when the seam shows on the outside of the garment. This seam cannot be used on a curved seamline. Try the seam first on a scrap of fabric to decide on the finished width. The finished seam width should be between ⅛ and ¼ (3 and 6mm). The lighter weight the fabric, the narrower the seam.

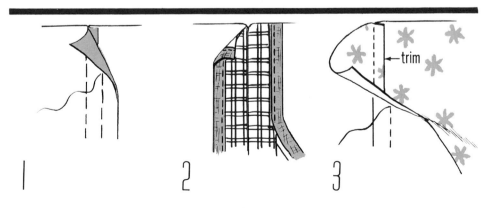

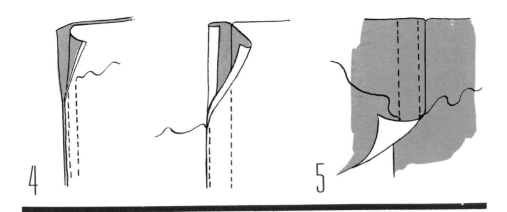

4

5

With wrong sides of fabric together, stitch seam at ⅜ inch (1cm) for a ¼-inch (6-mm) seam, or at ½ inch (1.3cm) for a ⅛-inch (3-mm) seam. Trim seam allowances to a scant ⅛ inch (3mm), and press together to one side. Turn garment, and with right sides together, press on first seamline. Stitch on wrong side ¼ or ⅛ inch (6 or 3mm) from first seam. The combined measurements for the two seams should total ⅝ inch (1.5cm).

MOCK FRENCH SEAM

The mock French seam can be substituted for the French seam on curved seamlines where the French seam cannot be used. This seam can be made in two ways. Make a plain seam on the wrong side of the garment first. Then either (1) stitch the two seam allowances together ¼ inch (6mm) from seamline, and trim, leaving ⅛ or ¹⁄₁₆-inch (3 to 1.5-mm) edge beyond second line of stitching; or (2) trim seam allowances if too wide, press together with edges turned inside, and stitch along the folded edges.

LAPPED SEAM

The lapped seam is often used on leather and suede for a neat finish. Trim seam allowance from what will be the upper side. Lap one seam allowance over the other so the seamlines meet. Secure seam with double-faced adhesive, if necessary. Topstitch seam along trimmed edge. Topstitch again ¼ inch (6mm) from first seam to complete the lapped seam.

Always turn up hems before turning back facing edges at front opening or side vents of a shirt. The area that shows will appear finished. A shirt or shirt jacket worn outside pants or skirts will look and hang better if the hem is finished 1 or 2 inches (2.5 or 5cm) deep. The exception: For a soft look in some fabrics and styles, a narrow hem is used instead.

Shirts to be worn tucked in are finished with a narrow hem appropriate for the fabric. The hem should not show through garment.

HEM WITH STAYSTITCHED EDGE

On heavy fabrics—corduroy, for example—or fabrics that do not ravel, such as knits, when the shirt will be worn inside, the hem edge may be staystitched ⅝ inch (1.5cm) from edge and pinked or zigzag stitched along the raw edge.

NARROW HEM FOR KNITS

When the shirt is to be worn outside, many hems on knits simply can be topstitched. Staystitch ⅝ inch (1.5cm) from edge. Turn seam allowance to underside on staystitching line, press, and topstitch hem ⅜ inch (1cm) from fold. For a knit shirt with curved openings at side seams, topstitching across the top of opening will act as reinforcement for this area and give a nice continuation to the line of topstitching. Embroidered arrowheads would be a nice touch here (see pages 77–78).

NARROW SHIRT HEM

On lightweight fabrics staystitch ¼ inch (6mm) from lower edge. Turn raw edge on staystitching line, turn up a narrow hem, and stitch at machine along upper edge. You may wish to add a second row of topstitching along lower edge to give more firmness.

For a very fine finish, after staystitching and turning in raw edge on staystitching line you may prefer to slipstitch hem by hand.

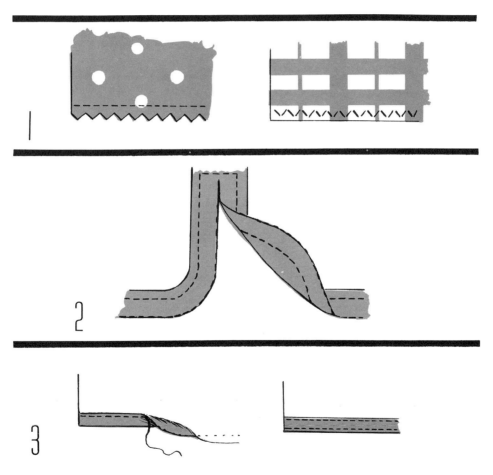

WIDE HEM

A wide hem should be between 1 and 2 inches (2.5 and 5cm) deep. Use an automatic hem gauge to turn up hem to correct finished length; press. Staystitch hem ¼ inch (6mm) from edge. On fabric that does not ravel leave edge raw, or pink if you wish. Hem by hand, using a tailor's hem. With garment and hem facing you, turn back hem edge about ¼ inch (6mm). Working from right to left, take a small stitch first in the turned back hem edge just above the fold, as shown; then insert needle at an angle into garment, and take a very small stitch. Angle needle again to take another small stitch in hem edge. Continue around shirt, spacing stitches no more than ½ inch (1.3cm) apart for a secure hem.

If fabric requires a finish, staystitch ¼ inch (6mm) from raw edge. Turn edge under on staystitching, and clean finish by stitching close to fold. Hem with a tailor's hem or a machine-stitched hem.

A ¼-inch (6-mm) strip of fusible material also works well for many medium to heavyweight fabrics. Insert barely under upper edge of turned-up hem. Use steam to press securely to fabric. On a heavy fabric, to melt bonding material much faster, place metal hem gauge or aluminum foil on press board under garment.

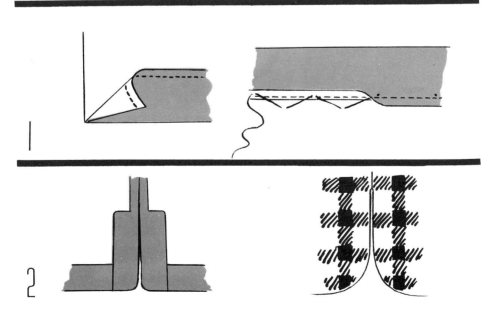

If you would like vents (side openings) and the pattern does not have them, add 1 inch (2.5cm) beyond the seam allowance for the depth of the opening you desire. If you would like to curve the vent, you can simply round off the square ends. Side openings are slenderizing, curved ones even more so. However, a really deep curve will give the opposite effect, making the wearer appear "hippy." Look at the illustration.

CURVED VENTS AT SIDE SEAMS
If you desire more support for these vents than is given by the narrow shirt hem, use a fitted facing. For shirts and shirt jackets, to eliminate bulk over the hips it may be desirable to use a lightweight fabric for the facing instead of self-fabric.

SHIRTTAIL WITH DEEP CURVES
A deep curve at the hemline is popular but not as slenderizing as curved vents. This deep curve can be finished with a fitted facing or with one of the narrow hems.

SQUARE-FINISHED VENTS
Square-finished, or straight, vents at side seams give a shirt worn outside a soft look. To make straight vents allow 1 inch (2.5cm) on each seam allowance the depth of opening for finishing. Finish the hem first, and turn back the facing over it, slipstitching the latter in position as shown. This is the same finish used to turn the front facings of a shirt back over the hem.

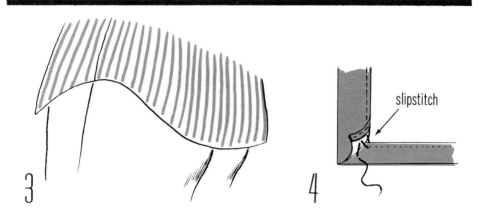

3

4

slipstitch

SHIRTBANDS

Use a shirtband for a classic, tailored shirt look. The vertical line of the band is flattering to many figures. The shirtband without a facing is used with the collar with a neckband, the band with a foldback facing with a one-piece collar.

MOCK SHIRTBAND

Making a mock shirtband is simply a matter of cutting extra fabric onto the shirt front as you cut it and then pressing it in position. The band replaces interfacing.

Cut the right front (left front for men) from **a** to **b** as shown. Unpin the pattern. Multiply by four the distance on the pattern between center front and facing foldline; mark this distance from **a** and **b** at **c** and **d** on your fabric, and cut from **a** to **c** and from **b** to **d**. Replace the pattern with the foldline on **d** and **c.** Cut the facing between **c** and **d,** as shown.

Turn facing to underside, and press with foldline over center front line, as shown. Then press creased band back over right side of shirt front. Buttonholes will hold the band in place.

SHIRTBAND WITH FOLDBACK FACING

The shirtband with facing is used with a one-piece collar. Fold the facing back on foldline; press. Cut band 2½ inches (6.5cm) wide. Always cut band on lengthwise grain. (If cut on bias, the band may ripple.)

Staystitch edges of band if necessary to turn fabric easily on seamline. Fold to wrong side and press a ½-inch (1.3-cm) seam allowance on each side of band. Interface band between seam allowances if fabric requires. Place band right side out on right (left for men) shirt front so that it extends ⅛ inch (3mm) beyond foldline. Topstitch ¼ inch (6mm) from each edge of band. Do not catch facing in the inside row of topstitching. Proceed with collar.

SHIRTBAND WITHOUT FACING

Make this band if your shirt collar has a neckband. Cut the right front (left front for men) to extend ½ inch (1.3cm) beyond the foldline for facing. Staystitch edge if necessary. Turn and press this ½-inch (1.3-cm) seam allowance to right side. Cut band, interface, press, and stitch to shirt by the method described for Shirtband with Foldback Facing.

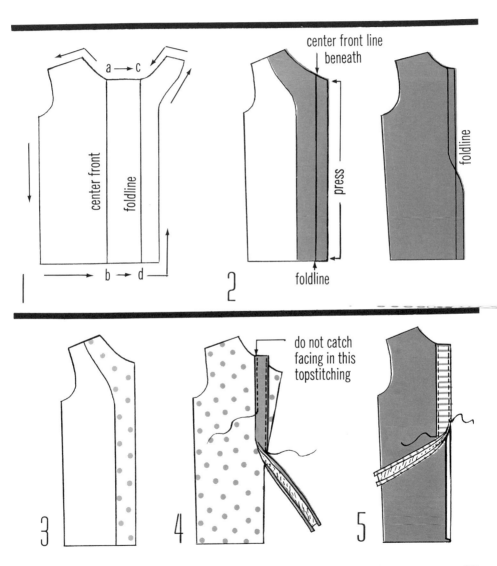

POLO OPENINGS

Polo openings can easily be constructed using the directions that follow instead of those on your pattern instruction sheet. These openings will be much more professional-looking, and they are much easier to make. Use the strips described instead of cutting the pieces that come with your pattern.

The length of the opening is up to you. A man's shirt opening should be about 9 inches (23cm), a child's garment 4 to 7 inches (10 to 18cm), and a woman's dress opening can be anywhere from 10 to 22 inches (25.5 to 56cm).

Cut the shirt front on a fold at center front. On inside of garment mark center front line the desired length of the opening. Next mark a line ¾ inch (2cm) on either side of the center front. [The polo opening will be 1½ inches (3.8cm) wide.]

POLO OPENING FOR LIGHTWEIGHT FABRIC

Cut or tear a lengthwise piece of fabric wide enough to extend to the shoulder seams, 12 inches (30.5cm) or more, and 2 inches (5cm) longer than the desired opening. (Striped fabric should be cut on the crosswise grain for an attractive trim.) This is for the welt. Place fabric on garment, right sides together, with center of welt fabric on center front line of garment (see illustration). With garment wrong side up stitch from neckline down one marking line, straight across the bottom of opening, and up the second marking line to the neckline. Use small stitches ½ inch (1.3cm) on either side of corners. Slash center front line to a point ¾ inch (2cm) from bottom of opening. Clip at an angle to each corner. Trim each seam allowance to ¼ inch (6mm), and press seam allowances away from center front.

On outside of garment the right welt will lap over the left on women's shirts; for men's shirts the overlap is reversed. Fold and press the side that will be the under welt on true grain so it perfectly meets the opposite edge of opening. Use strips of press-on interfacing on welts between foldlines to give body if needed. Pin under welt in place. On underside of front, stitch welt in position over first line of stitches, as shown. Make the overlap welt in the same way. Turn both welts to inside of shirt front. Be sure welts lap in correct direction. Smooth and pin in position. On right side finish the lower edge with a triangle or square of stitching (see illustration). Cut away extra fabric below triangle on underside.

POLO OPENING FOR MEDIUM TO HEAVY FABRIC
In medium to heavy fabric—double knit, for example—face the opening with lightweight fabric. Press two lengthwise or crosswise strips for the opening. Place them in position, and stitch as described for polo opening with lightweight fabric. Make collar.

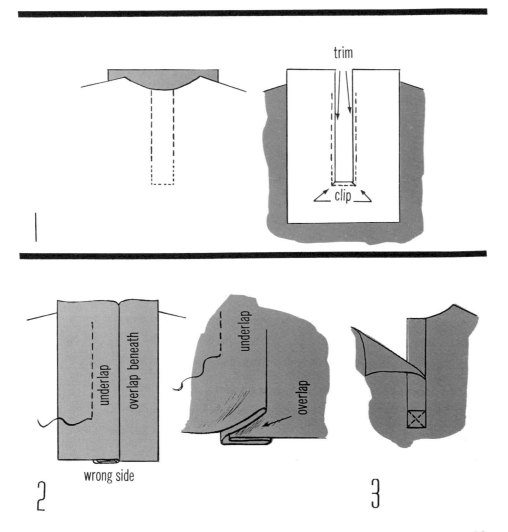

trim

clip

1

underlap

overlap beneath

wrong side

2

underlap

overlap

3

OTHER SPECIAL SHIRT TECHNIQUES

FACING EDGE CUT ON SELVAGE

Using selvage as a facing edge eliminates the need to finish the facing. It also gives more body to the shirt front, which is desirable except for large bust sizes.

Measure to find the widest part of the facing, **a,** between foldline and facing edge. Pin the pattern to fabric this distance from selvage, keeping straight of grain mark on true grain. Cut fabric except along facing edge, which will be the selvage. Do not attempt to cut the curve into the facing edge.

STITCHING A CURVED YOKE SEAM

Pattern instruction sheets often state that a curved yoke seam should be stitched from the top of the garment, but it is impossible to obtain a perfect curved line in this way. This seam may be top-stitched to finish, but do not apply the curved yoke with a top-stitched lapped seam.

For perfection and ease of stitching a curved seam, first staystitch the inside (concave) curve, **a,** precisely on the seamline; clip at intervals to staystitching. Stitch outside (convex) curve, **b,** ½ inch (1.3cm) from edge. Place the inside curve over outside curve, matching raw edges, right sides of fabric together. Stitch seam one thread inside staystitching. Press seam toward yoke. Top-stitch, if desired.

TURN-OF-CLOTH

The turn-of-cloth principle can be applied whenever two layers of cloth are stitched together. The outer layer must always have more ease to turn and finish smoothly over the under layer. Otherwise the under layer will tend to show after it has been stitched and turned. In the case of collars, the under collar should be trimmed on the outside edges ⅛ inch (3mm) on lightweight fabrics and slightly more on medium and heavy fabrics.

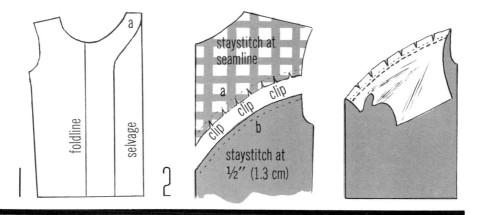

GRADED SEAMS

In some constructions—joining facings to a garment made from heavy fabric, for example—the bulk of seam can be reduced by grading. Press the seam open. Trim interfacing, if any, close to seamline. One seam allowance—the one that is to rest against the outside of garment—is trimmed to ¼ inch (6mm); the other seam allowance is trimmed to ⅛ (3mm). This reduces bulk, and the wider allowance serves as a cushion for the narrower, preventing its showing from outside of garment.

TOPSTITCHING ON BUTTON SIDE OF FACING

A row of topstitching through center front on the button side of the shirt will give an exact line for placement of buttons and will hold the facing in perfect position when the shirt is laundered. Except on a print (unlikely to show) end the stitching at the top button.

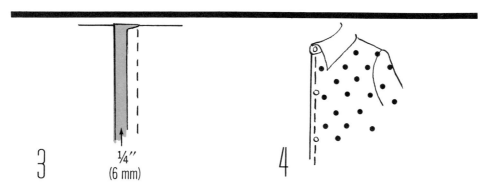

TUNNEL WAISTLINE

To make a tunnel at the waistline for a drawstring or belt, cut a lengthwise strip of fabric the desired width for the belt plus ¼ inch (6mm) seam allowance on each side. Staystitch strip ¼ inch (6mm) from each edge; turn and press edges on staystitching line. Stitch casing to inside of shirt. Insert drawstring or belt in tunnel. Try on shirt, and distribute fullness where it is most attractive on the figure. Usually fullness is most flattering in two groups front and back, in much the same positions as waistline darts. Pin adjusted fullness in place (**a, b, c, d** in illustration). Stitch to hold adjusted fullness in position.

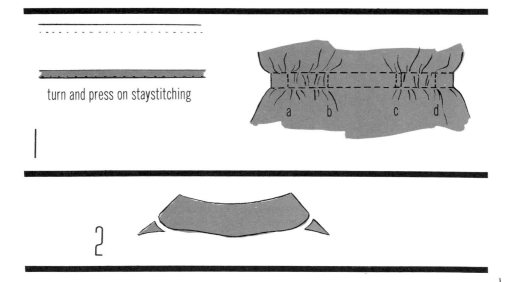

turn and press on staystitching

a   b   c   d

MAKING CURVES FROM POINTS

If your fabric is bulky, rounding corners on collars and cuffs will make it easier to stitch, turn, and press them.

MAKING BODY SHIRTS FROM SHIRTS

You can make a shirt you are constructing into a body shirt. You can also apply the same method to shirts in your wardrobe that are difficult to keep tucked into pants or skirts. Instead of making the briefs, you may prefer to buy a pair to use for making your body shirt. Cut off the elastic at the top, and open the front seam of the crotch. Proceed as for briefs made from pattern.

Cut 3 inches (7.5cm) from the top of a panty pattern. Cut the panty and crotch piece from nylon tricot. Make certain the crosswise grain (the direction of greatest stretch for tricot) is vertical.

Make briefs according to pattern instruction sheet, but do not attach the front of the crotch piece to the front of the briefs. These opening edges can be finished with pieces of snap tape or with a piece of ½-inch (1.3-cm) twill tape if you use plain snaps. The body shirt is much easier to fasten from back to front.

Wear shirt, and slide briefs over the shirttail. Pin the two layers together; sit down to check for length. Remove garment; trim excess length from shirt; leave ¼-inch (6-mm) seam allowance. Stitch the seam; press and topstitch or zigzag edges of seam allowance together to keep seam flat unless shirt fabric is bulky. If so, press seam open, and zigzag each edge to shirt. This will keep the edges flat. For heavier fabrics you may prefer to overlap shirt on briefs and zigzag with two rows of stitching, instead of making a seam and pressing it open.

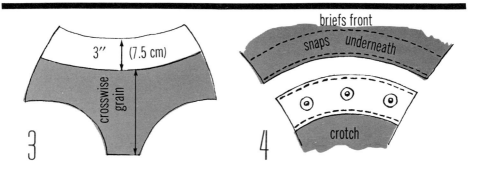

ASCOTS AND TIES

An ascot or soft bow at the neckline can completely change the silhouette. Following are three methods for making either.

BIAS TRICK ASCOT OR TIE

The bias trick ascot or tie can be made in a single color or in any combination your imagination dictates. The trick of this tie is in the stitching. There is no pattern. The tie can be any width or length. When stitching is completed the tie will be approximately two-thirds as wide and two-thirds as long as the piece you cut.

Use a strip or strips of fabric from either the lengthwise or crosswise grain. If you wish to make a two-color or some other combination of tie, make two strips, each half as wide as the piece you wish to start with, plus seam allowances. Seam them together along one edge. Trim, press seam open. Place fabric right side up. Fold one end of the sash on the diagonal until it meets the long edge, **d,** on the other side. Pin at **b** as shown, ¼ inch (6mm) from edge. Stitch from point, **a,** of triangle to base, **b.**

With needle in fabric exactly at **b,** remove pin. Lift presser foot; pivot; stitch to end of strip, continuing to bring edge **c** to edge **d** all the way down. Press seam open on edge presser. Turn tie to right side, and close end by slipstitching. The straight strip will now lie on the bias, and the seam will spiral around the length.

TRUE BIAS TIE OR ASCOT

To make a bias tie or ascot in which the seam groove is hidden in the edge, begin with a piece of fabric cut on true bias. It should be the length desired, and twice the width desired, plus seam allowances.

Fold fabric in half and make nicks with the scissors about every six inches. Match the nicks as you stitch along the long edge. The tie will not roll; matching nicks will insure that you do not stretch fabric edges out of shape. Leave an opening in seam large enough to turn tie right side out. Stitch both ends on machine. Press seam allowances open before turning tie right side out. Slip-stitch opening; press seam flat, but do not press bias folded edge.

74

TIE FROM A SINGLE LAYER

Do not hem a single-layer tie or ascot by machine if you desire a look of quality. Staystitch ⅛ to ¼ inch (3 to 6mm) from edge to be hemmed. Trim edge to within a few threads of staystitching.

Turn fabric twice to conceal raw edges. Hold fabric firmly in left hand (right hand if you are left-handed). With needle in other hand push out width of rolled hem until it is less than ⅛ inch (3mm) deep. Slipstitch, using a fine needle and single thread. Run needle in fold of hem ¼ inch (6mm), slide needle down, and pick a thread in garment; bring needle out under hem. Slide needle in hem again at same distance; continue slipstitching around hem.

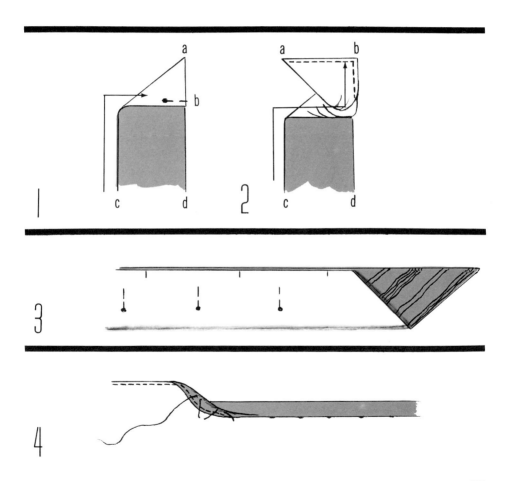

TRIMS

BRAIDS, SEQUINS, LACE

Look carefully at your shirt and consider ways to dress it up or down. Even denim shirts have been trimmed with rows of sequins or beading. Outline edge of yoke, pockets, collar, cuffs, shirtband, or any combination of these. Several rows of trim can be used down the front on either side of band to emphasize the vertical lines and the shirt length.

APPLIQUÉS

Here are some great tricks to help you add appliqués wherever you choose:

☆ For garment that will be laundered, shrink purchased appliqués before applying to garment.

☆ Use a dramatic paisley, a bold abstract, or a whimsical print as a source for an original appliqué. Zigzag stitch a piece of the fabric to your garment, outlining the design; then cut around the design. This preserves the line and grain of fabric without distortion.

☆ Place a small piece of bonding material under the appliqué; press on shirt to hold appliqué in perfect position for stitching it to the shirt.

☆ Zigzag or embroider around the edge to apply.

☆ On large appliqués use two rows of zigzag stitching — a narrow stitch around the edge and a wider one just inside the first row of stitches.

☆ You might stitch sequins to an appliqué before applying it, if the garment will be drycleaned only.

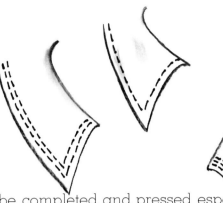

TOPSTITCHING

Edges to be topstitched should be completed and pressed especially carefully. After topstitching press the stitched area again. For a quality look, use a moderately long stitch, a loose tension, and a slower-than-normal stitching speed. With heavy thread use a large needle. There are many ways to achieve effects with topstitching:

- ☆ Thread the machine with two or three bobbins of thread on the top. Use a needle-threader, if necessary, to thread them through the machine needle.
- ☆ Use a spool of heavy duty thread for the needle thread only.
- ☆ Use a spool of buttonhole twist for the needle thread only.
- ☆ Always use regular thread on the bobbin.
- ☆ Try several rows of topstitching ⅛ to ¼ inch (3 to 6mm) apart. (One famous American designer has used several rows of zigzagging as topstitching.)
- ☆ Use contrasting color or colors for topstitching. Gold or silver thread can be used for a dressy touch. Try black, brown, or navy on white. Echo a subordinate color in a print.

ARROWHEADS

Arrowheads are popular for reinforcing vents at side seams, pocket ends, inside buttonhole edges or to add trim, as at the point of a dart. These are especially good for the Western look.

1. Draw or baste a triangle in correct position on garment. An average arrowhead is about ⅝ inch (1.5cm) at base; make yours larger or smaller as needed. Use a hand stitch and a single thread. Insert needle from underside of garment near

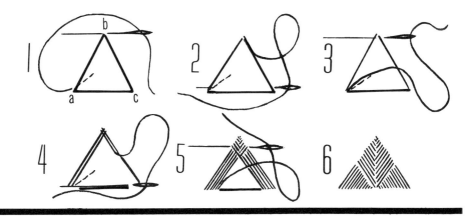

center of triangle. Take a few running stitches, and bring
needle out on right side at corner **a.** Insert needle at point **b,**
and take one tiny stitch from right to left.

2. Insert needle at point **c,** and bring it out as close as possible
to the first stitch at point **a.**
3. Insert needle at point **b** again, as close as possible under the
first stitch. Bring out on marked line at the left.
4. Return needle to point **c;** insert just to left of first stitch. It
should emerge just to right of last stitch at **a.**
5,6. Repeat procedures above, taking each stitch close to the
previous one. Continue until the triangle is filled. Anchor
thread on underside before clipping.

IT'S ELEMENTARY FOR THE SHIRT LOOK

PREPARATION
CUTTING
MARKING
STITCHING

GRAINLINE

Cutting, fitting, stitching, and pressing are directed to making a garment that is grain-perfect. Grain perfection is vital if a garment is to keep its shape and appearance, because grain always seeks its true position. A garment can hang, wear, and fit beautifully only when grain-perfect.

Warp yarns compose the lengthwise grain of the fabric; the filling, or weft, yarns make up the crosswise grain. If the warp and filling yarns lie at right angles to each other, the grain is true. If they do not lie at right angles, the fabric is off-grain.

Lengthwise grain of woven fabric is usually strongest and has the greatest amount of stability. Crosswise grain has a slight amount of give. True bias, which has the greatest amount of stretch, lies at a 45-degree angle to the true grain.

Knitted fabrics do not have warp and filling threads. The vertical rib of a knit fabric is called the wale; it is comparable to the crosswise grain of woven fabric. The greatest stretch in most knits is in the crosswise grain.

STRAIGHTEN ENDS OF FABRIC

If a garment is to be made on grain, the fabric must be on grain before the garment pieces are cut. The way to find if your fabric is on-grain and the first steps to straightening off-grain fabric are the same: Make each of the crosswise ends straight, with the end crosswise thread running from selvage to selvage. The method depends on fabric.

Many, but not all, fabrics can be torn. Linen, many wools, fabrics with heavy or rough threads, most nap-surfaced fabrics, and knits will not tear well.

If you have a fabric that will tear, clip a selvage with your scissors as far down as appears necessary to straighten the end. Hold each side of the clipped edge firmly, and give a quick pull. The fabric should tear across to the other selvage, which you then will need to cut across. It is necessary to tear quickly and firmly to avoid a lengthwise split in the material. If you have any doubts as to your success, use one of the other methods. Press raw edges to flatten ripples and restore grainline.

Drawing or pulling a thread is another way to straighten crosswise ends of fabric. Find a thread that goes all the way across; carefully pull it until the fabric puckers and you can see the threadline distinctly. Cut the fabric along this line to straighten each end.

On some fabrics it will not be possible to pull a thread all the way across, but you can ravel the crosswise threads until you have a straight thread across the width of fabric. Cut off raveled threads.

If a fabric has a woven design such as a plaid or crosswise stripe, cut along one of the lines of the design.

corner of a table. (You can also use the corner of your cutting board, or the right angle of a T-square.) If the grain is straight, or true, one crosswise edge will lie straight against the other side of the right angle, the folded edge will lie flat, and the surface of the fabric will be smooth.

If this is not the case, you will need to straighten the fabric grain before cutting out the pattern pieces. In most cases straightening the grain can be combined with the process of preshrinking your fabric. After your fabric has been processed and the grain straightened, it should be kept folded accordion-fashion on the true grain until it is ready for use.

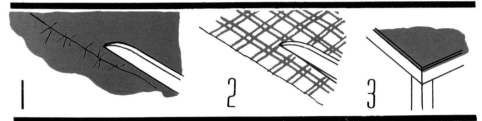

However, be sure that the fabric design is woven. Designs that are printed on fabric may be off grain.

To straighten the crosswise ends of a knit fabric, fold the fabric in half lengthwise, making sure the foldline is on a lengthwise rib. Use a T-square, or place the lengthwise grain against one side of a square table or your cutting board. Mark straight across the crosswise end with chalk, and cut along mark.

CHECK GRAIN POSITION When both ends of the fabric have been straightened, you will be able to determine the grain position of the threads. Fold the fabric lengthwise with the selvages together, smoothing the fabric toward the fold. Line up the selvage straight against the

PRESHRINK FABRIC/STRAIGHTEN GRAIN It is a general rule that washable fabrics and most wools should be preshrunk before cutting. Prepare the fabric by perfecting the crosswise ends, then fold, right sides together, and baste the selvages and the two crosswise ends. The fabric is ready for preshrinking. This is an important step, because even a small amount of shrinkage can alter the fit of a garment enough to ruin the effect you are working to obtain. Remember to preshrink all other parts of a garment that will be laundered — interfacings, if woven, zippers, and any other notions.

If you will launder your garment, wash the fabric before cutting exactly as you will wash the completed garment. This means that you must

81

read care labels carefully for information concerning the fabric and its performance. You must know at what temperatures your fabric can be washed and how to dry it.

Use the same soap you will use, and wash and dry the fabric at the same temperature as you will the garment. (The automatic dryer, as well as the washing process, can cause shrinkage.) If the garment is to be drip-dried and the fabric is a knit, be careful to support the length so it will not stretch. (The weight of a wet length of several yards of fabric will be much greater than that of your completed garment, and your garment will be supported by seams.) You can begin to press when the fabric is damp-dry if you need to straighten the grain.

If your fabric is washable but you intend to dryclean the garment (as you might linen, for example), prepare by basting; then press the fabric with a steam iron, straightening the grain, if necessary.

Although they will be drycleaned, all wool fabrics should be pre-shrunk, because steam pressing will shrink them. Some wools will have been preshrunk when you buy them. If your fabric has not been, preshrink it. If it is not grain-perfect, you will need to straighten the grain after preshrinking. Preshrink and straighten the grain as follows.

Baste the fabric, folded lengthwise with right sides together. Snip the selvages at intervals. Prepare processing cloths from old sheets or any clean, absorbent, nonfading cotton fabric that will hold moisture well. The cloths should be several inches wider than the fabric folded lengthwise, and they should be as long as the fabric. (To insure enough length several pieces can be sewed together, or they can simply be laid end to end, so long as the ends meet.) Wet these cloths thoroughly and remove excess water, leaving the cloths damp.

Use a large piece of plastic to protect the surface on which you lay the cloths. Spread the damp cloths over the plastic on a flat surface, and center the wool — folded lengthwise, right sides together, basted — on them. Fold wool and cloths together evenly from both ends toward the center in several folds. Press on the folds with your hands to be sure that the moisture penetrates the layers. Cover with the plastic to help retain and distribute the moisture. Leave for two to four hours; then remove the fabric, unfold, and lay it on a flat surface. Smooth and pull it gently with your hands until it is grain-perfect. When the wool is almost dry on one side, turn it to the other to shrink it evenly. Use steam to press on the lengthwise grain and straighten grain if necessary.

SHRINK NOTIONS Woven interfacings, belting, ribbons, trims, even zippers, if they are to be used on washable garments, should be preshrunk before the garment is made. Be sure they are wet thoroughly; then dry, and press if necessary.

FABRICS THAT NEED NOT BE PRESHRUNK An off-grain fabric that does not require preshrinking can often be straightened by steam pressing. Baste the two selvages together after your fabric has been folded lengthwise with the right sides together. Match the folded fabric at each end; then baste across the two matched ends. The fabric will not lie smoothly if it is off-grain.

Test press your fabric. See Pressing and pressing charts, pages 92–96. Dampen the fabric on the underside with a sponge or damp cloth, and press carefully along the lengthwise grain, moving from the selvage to the fold. Be careful not to press the fold; this would make a crease that would be difficult to remove. Smooth the fabric with your hands as you work, and keep the fabric square with the grain at all times. If the fabric is extremely off-grain, this method may not straighten it.

It may be easier to correct the grain on shorter lengths of fabric. Cut the fabric into lengths on which major pattern pieces will fit. This technique does not require more fabric, and it will help greatly to achieve grain perfection in cutting.

DOUBLE KNITS If a polyester double knit garment is to be washed, the fabric should be preshrunk. Polyester double knits to be drycleaned need not be. To straighten double knits straighten the crosswise ends; baste; then straighten the grain as for a woven fabric, by pressing. Be sure your iron is at the right setting for your fabric when pressing.

LAMINATED KNITS AND FABRICS WITH PERMANENT FINISHES Laminated knits, commonly called bonded knits, and fabrics with permanent press or crease-resistant finishes, polished cottons and chintzes will have threads locked in a permanent position. If these are off-grain, they cannot be straightened. If you use such a fabric, place the straight-of-the-grain markings of the pattern on the straight of the design rather than the grainline. Do this for each individual pattern piece. If the fabric does not have a design, sometimes you can align each pattern piece separately on the straight of grain.

Permanent finishes with a fishy smell should be washed with a detergent in a regular wash cycle.

CUTTING AND MARKING

Cutting-to-fit is a technique for altering the measurement of your garment pieces to fit while cutting out the fabric. See pages 97–102. If you must alter your pattern, take this into consideration while laying out pattern pieces in order to allow the necessary additional inches for each garment piece that you must alter.

Lay out and check all the pattern pieces against the layout guide. Be sure you have allowed space for any necessary alterations. When cutting knits use the wale of the fabric as the lengthwise grain. If a knit has a fold that cannot be pressed out, place your pattern pieces in such a way as to avoid the fold, or place it on a part of the garment— under the arm, for example—where it will not be conspicuous.

It is helpful to cut extra notches on pattern and fabric pieces. The top of the sleevecap by the shoulder seam mark and the center fold of a shirt back that will be joined to a yoke are two examples of places where extra notches are useful.

Use tracing paper and wheel to transfer pattern marks to the wrong side of garment pieces, and use thread tracing (basting through a single layer) for marks that must be visible on right side of garment.

MACHINE STITCHING

Regulation stitches are used for the permanent stitching of seams, darts, and other garment details. The length of permanent stitches can vary depending on the fabric. See charts, pages 87–91, for suggested stitch length for various fabrics.

Staystitching is regulation-length stitching done in the direction of the grain before a garment piece is joined to another. It is usually done a thread outside the seamline, in the seam allowance, unless instructions call for stitching at a different distance from the seam. Staystitching is used on any area of a garment that is more than slightly off-grain or that requires further construction. It prevents these edges of garment pieces from stretching during construction.

Baste stitching is done with the longest machine stitch (6–8). It is used to hold two layers of fabric together before permanent stitching them. You may want to do this for fitting a garment. Basting is also useful in difficult areas of construction, or if fabric is hard to stitch for some reason. Basting is sometimes used as a guide for other stitching.

Grain direction can usually be seen by the position of fabric threads at raw edges. The threads lie smooth and straight along cut edges in direction of the grain. Against the grain they appear curled back, rough, and uneven. Basting, staystitching, and regulation stitching should be done in direction of the grain, except for edges that are cut on the straight or almost-straight of either lengthwise or crosswise grain. These can be stitched in either direction. See the illustrations for directional stitching to maintain true grain in your garment pieces.

HAND STITCHES

Choose needle and thread. To thread a needle, cut thread at an angle with sharp scissors. This makes a clean, sharp end that goes through the eye of the needle easily. Always work with a single strand of thread. Coat thread with beeswax, and run a warm iron over it to keep it from knotting. Thread needle with end of thread that was cut from spool. The same end should be knotted before beginning to sew.

BAR TACKS Bar tacks can be made by hand, as well as by machine. To make them by hand, take three or four stitches of the length required in the same place, inserting needle through fabric each time. Then, beginning at one end of the long stitches, take small overhand stitches over the three or four threads, catching some of the fabric underneath as you do so, until the first stitches are entirely covered. Finish each end of the bar with a smaller bar stitched perpendicular to it if you like.

BASTING Hand basting can be used instead of machine basting when a delicate fabric is apt to show marks from machine basting. Use thread of a contrasting color and large, straight stitches. Stitch a thread outside the seamline in the seam allowance. At the beginning and end of stitching use short backstitches to secure basting. A variation is a long stitch on one side of fabric and a short on the other.

OVERCAST Overcasting can be used to keep raw edges of seams from raveling. Stitch at a slant, using large, even, closely spaced stitches.

RUNNING STITCH The length of these stitches will depend on the fabric and on the purpose of the stitches. To hand stitch sheer or delicate fabrics, use a $1/16$-inch (1.5-mm) stitch. For medium to heavy fabrics, use a $1/8$-inch (3-mm) stitch. Use a $1/4$-inch (6-mm) stitch for hand gathering. Insert needle in fabric, push it through with thimble, and draw thread through. Be sure to keep fabric flat, and do not allow thread to pucker fabric. Repeat procedure.

1

2

3   4

5   6

85

SLIPSTITCH The slipstitch can be used to join two edges without the stitches showing; however, it is not a strong stitch and should not be used in an area that will be subject to strain. For hems, it will scarcely be visible on the garment or the hem side. (Do not use it for hems with heavy fabrics.) Insert needle first into underside of hem fold and then into garment, picking up only a single thread in the garment side. Draw needle and thread through; repeat.

WHIPSTITCH The whipstitch is stronger than the slipstitch and can be substituted for it to hold together edges that will be subject to strain. It might be used to attach inside edges of cuffs to sleeves, or the center back of a collar to a shirt when the fabric is bulky or heavy or when the garment will receive hard wear.

Insert needle through upper edge, hiding knot beneath edge. Place point of needle in opposite side, as near as possible to the first edge. With point of needle under edge, move needle ahead, bringing it up through the first edge. Repeat procedure. The stitches should be so small they scarcely can be seen.

STITCHING SPECIAL FABRICS

The following charts give recommendations for stitching a number of types of fabrics. In general, the lighter the fabric, the finer the needle should be, and the heavier or denser the fabric, the coarser the needle. Size 9 machine needles are extra fine; 11, fine; 14, medium; 16, coarse; 18, extra coarse.

If your fabric is not listed in the stitching charts, use the following as a general guide for needle, thread, and stitch length. To learn if any special handling is necessary, make a sample seam and observe how the fabric behaves.

FABRIC WEIGHT	VERY LIGHT	LIGHT	MEDIUM	MEDIUM HEAVY	HEAVY
EXAMPLE	ciré	gingham	linen	flannel	duck
NEEDLE	9	9, 11	11, 14	14, 16	16, 18
STITCH LENGTH	16–20	12–16	10–14	8–12	6–10
MERCERIZED COTTON	fine	50	50	50 or heavy duty	heavy duty
SILK	"A"	"A"	"A"	"A"	
POLYESTER/COTTON	X	X	X	X	X
POLYESTER	X	X	X	heavy duty	heavy duty
NYLON		nylon tricot	X	X	X

Note: An X indicates that the appropriate thread comes in only one size.

FABRIC	NEEDLE	THREAD	STITCH LENGTH
CORDUROY AND VELVETEEN	14	mercerized	8–10 per inch
CREPE	11	mercerized; silk for topstitching	10–12
DENIM	14, 16	heavy duty mercerized	8–12
DOUBLE KNIT	11, 14 sharp or ball-point	mercerized........machine stretch poly/cot*, polyester....zigzag or regular all, 10–12	
DURABLE PRESS	11–14	mercerized or poly/cot*	heavy, 8–10 light, 10–14
FELT	14, sharp	mercerized	8–10
JERSEY	9–11, sharp or ball-point	polyester or poly/cot*	12–14
LACE	11	mercerized, poly/cot,* or silk, according to fabric	10–12
LEATHER AND SUEDE	leather 11–16	heavy-duty mercerized, polyester, or silk	8–10
LEATHERLIKE AND VINYL	leather 14–16	polyester poly/cot*	8–10

* Polyester/cotton

† NOTES FOR SPECIAL HANDLING
1. Use a roller foot.
2. Stitch with tissue paper between presser foot and fabric.
3. Stitch with tissue between throatplate and fabric.
4. Cover the throatplate hole with a piece of adhesive tape.
5. Place a piece of adhesive or cellophane tape around the toes of your regular presser foot.
6. With a zigzag or straight stitch, hold the fabric in front and in back of the presser foot firmly enough to stretch it (keep it taut) as you sew. Hold the fabric to its true maximum length without stretching out of shape. You will not need this technique if you have a stretch stitch on your machine. Sometimes a fine zigzag stitch with polyester thread will provide enough give. Make a sample seam, and stretch it. If the stitching breaks, you need to stretch as you sew.

TENSION	PRESSURE	† NOTES FOR SPECIAL HANDLING	SEAM FINISH
slightly relaxed	average, but test	11, 12	edgestitch
relaxed, but test	light	10, 12	zigzag or overcast
average	average to heavy	no special handling needed	no, unless flat-fell
average	average	6, 7	no
usually slightly relaxed	average, but test	3 or 4; 8	sometimes; pink or zigzag
slightly increased	slightly increased	13	no
test	average	3 or 4; 6	no, but edgestitch seams that roll
slightly relaxed	test	5, 10	French or mock French if seam will show
slightly relaxed	fairly light	7, 9, 13	glue or topstitch
average to slightly increased	light to average	1 or 2; 3, 13, 14	topstitch or glue (note difference for Suedelike, next page)

7. Stay seams that should not stretch—waistline or shoulder seams—with a piece of seam tape or yarn.
8. Hold fabric firmly in front and in back of the presser foot.
9. Be careful not to stretch while stitching.
10. Use both hands—one behind the presser foot to guide, not pull, the fabric under the needle.
11. Use your hand to separate the fabric layers in front of the needle.
12. Fabric may be slippery, or it may push ahead on the top layer. To prevent, baste before stitching.
13. Stitch carefully. If you baste, do so just in the seam allowance. The needle holes will not disappear if you remove stitching.
14. A special stitching tape with adhesive on one side and rows of parallel lines on the other is useful for topstitching. Stitch through tape, following lines; then remove tape when stitching is completed.

FABRIC	NEEDLE	THREAD	STITCH LENGTH
DIANA	11	polyester poly/cot * silk "A"	wovens, 10–12 more for knits
SATIN	11	mercerized polyester silk	12
SHEERS	9–11	fine	16
SILK	11	silk	light, 12–16 medium, 10–14
SUEDELIKE	leather 14–16	polyester silk	10–12, seams 5–8, ornamental
TRICOT	sharp or ball-point 9–11	polyester	12–15; fine, narrow zigzag, or 2 rows straight stitching
VELVET	11	mercerized silk	10–12; stitch in direction of nap

*Polyester/cotton

† NOTES FOR SPECIAL HANDLING
1. Use a roller foot.
2. Stitch with tissue paper between presser foot and fabric.
3. Stitch with tissue between throatplate and fabric.
4. Cover the throatplate hole with a piece of adhesive tape.
5. Place a piece of adhesive or cellophane tape around the toes of your regular presser foot.
6. With a zigzag or straight stitch, hold the fabric in front and in back of the presser foot firmly enough to stretch it (keep it taut) as you sew. Hold the fabric to its true maximum length without stretching out of shape. You will not need this technique if you have a stretch stitch on your machine. Sometimes a fine zigzag stitch with polyester thread will provide enough give. Make a sample seam, and stretch it. If the stitching breaks, you need to stretch as you sew.

TENSION	PRESSURE	†NOTES FOR SPECIAL HANDLING	SEAM FINISH
average	test	8	no
slightly relaxed	light	8, 13	if ravels, zigzag or overcast
light to average	light	soft sheers: 2 and/or 3; 10	French or mock French
usually slightly relaxed	light	12 and sometimes 13	sometimes: pink or zigzag
relaxed	test	1, 13; 2 for topstitching	do not use glue; topstitch or use heat-fusible adhesives
usually slightly relaxed	average	1, 4, 6	trim and stitch seam allowances together
usually slightly relaxed	light to average	12	no (garment should be lined)

7. Stay seams that should not stretch—waistline or shoulder seams—with a piece of seam tape or yarn.
8. Hold fabric firmly in front and in back of the presser foot.
9. Be careful not to stretch while stitching.
10. Use both hands—one behind the presser foot to guide, not pull, the fabric under the needle.
11. Use your hand to separate the fabric layers in front of the needle.
12. Fabric may be slippery, or it may push ahead on the top layer. To prevent, baste before stitching.
13. Stitch carefully. If you baste, do so just in the seam allowance. The needle holes will not disappear if you remove stitching.
14. A special stitching tape with adhesive on one side and rows of parallel lines on the other is useful for topstitching. Stitch through tape, following lines; then remove tape when stitching is completed.

FIBER	RIGHT SIDE	WRONG SIDE	NO HEAT		HEAT				
			FINGER PRESS	MALLET	VERY LOW	MEDIUM LOW	LOW	MEDIUM	HIGH
ACETATE	●	●			●●				
ACRYLIC		●				●			
COTTON	★	●							●
LINEN		●							●
NYLON		●	●		●				
NYLON BLENDS		●			SEE CARE LABEL				
POLYESTER		●						●	
QIANA	●	●						●	
RAYON		●				●			
SILK		●						●	
TRIACETATE		●				●			
VINYL/PLASTIC	★★★		●	●					
WOOL		●						●	

● STANDARD METHOD
● ALTERNATE METHOD
●● BOTH METHODS

SEE TEXT FOR DETAILS

PRESSING GUIDE

| STEAM | DRY | POUNDING BLOCK | TENSION | PROTECTION | | | | | | |
| | | | | OVER FABRIC | | | | UNDER FABRIC | | |
				PRESS CLOTH	PAPER STRIPS	TISSUE PAPER	BROWN PAPER	HEAVY TOWEL	NEEDLEBOARD	SELF-FABRIC
●				D						
●				D						
●	★			★						
●				●						
●				D						
TEST				●						
●				●						
●●			●	●						
●				●						
●				●		★★				
●				●						
	●									
●		●		●						

D/D Use dampened press cloth to steam press.

★ After steam pressing cotton, press until dry with dry iron; use press cloth when top pressing dark or textured cotton.

★★ Tissue may be needed under press cloth to prevent waterspotting.

★★★ Some vinyl and plastic-coated fabrics may be top pressed with a warm iron over a press cloth; see care label.

| FABRIC CONSTRUCTION | RIGHT SIDE | WRONG SIDE | NO HEAT | | HEAT | | | | |
			FINGER PRESS	MALLET	VERY LOW	MEDIUM LOW	LOW	MEDIUM	HIGH
CORDUROY/VELVETEEN		●			SEE FIBER				
CREPE		●			SEE FIBER				
DURABLE PRESS	★	●					●		★
DENIM		●			SEE FIBER				
FELT		●						●	
KNITS		●			SEE FIBER				
LACE		●			SEE FIBER				
LAMINATED/BONDED	●		●		SEE FIBER				
LEATHER/SUEDE		●●		●	●				
LEATHERLIKE/VINYL		●	●	●	★★				
NAPPED		●			SEE FIBER				
SATIN		●			SEE FIBER				
SUEDELIKE		●			●				
VELVET		●			SEE FIBER				

● STANDARD METHOD
● ALTERNATE METHOD
●● BOTH METHODS
SEE TEXT FOR DETAILS

STEAM	DRY	PROTECTION							
		OVER FABRIC				UNDER FABRIC			
		PRESS CLOTH	PAPER STRIPS	TISSUE PAPER	BROWN PAPER	HEAVY TOWEL	NEEDLEBOARD	BROWN PAPER	SELF-FABRIC
●		●				●	●		◉
	●	●				●			
★	●		●						
●									
	●	●	●						
●		●	●						
TEST		SEE FIBER				●			
●		●	●		◉			●	
	●	◉			●			●	
	★★	★★							
●	●	●				●			◉
TEST									
●		★★★	●			●			
●		★★★★					●		

★ When final pressing use highest temperature fiber will take and lots of steam.
★★ Some vinyls can be pressed on right side with a warm iron over a presscloth; see care label.
★★★ Use a mesh press cloth; press marks usually can be brushed off.
★★★★ Hold iron about 1 inch (2.5cm.) above fabric.

PRESSING

There are several basic rules to observe when pressing. The first is always test press a scrap of your fabric to determine the most effective temperature and see if the fabric shows iron shine or if it waterspots. You can avoid possible damage to your fashion fabric by taking a few minutes for test pressing.

Remember never to slide the iron across fabric. Lift the iron and set it down when you move it from one area to another. Always press with the grain to avoid distortion of garment lines. This is as important as preparing, cutting, and stitching the fabric on grain.

Use steam for construction pressing except when fiber or fabric prohibits. In cases where it is not possible to raise steam in the iron with the temperature setting required by the fiber or fabric, a dampened (never wet) press cloth can be used between the iron and fabric to provide moisture. A dampened press or cheesecloth can also be used to supply extra moisture as needed.

In addition to a drill press cloth, one of self-fabric is useful for pressing napped fabrics. There are some cases in which brown paper or tissue paper are useful as substitutes for a press cloth. In the case of silk, tissue paper can be used between iron and fabric to prevent waterspotting. Brown paper strips or strips of paper toweling should be used between such construction details as seam allowances, tucks, darts, and the fabric when pressing a fabric that marks easily. This helps prevent marks of the construction from showing on the right side of the garment.

The pounding block is used to pound steam into heavy fabric to mold it, and for flattening seams, pleats, and edges in heavy and resilient fabrics such as wool.

For leather and suede use brown paper over and under the fabric when you press. The top layer protects the fabric, and the paper underneath prevents small pieces of rough leather from clinging to your press board.

An attachment for irons is available at notions counters. It eliminates the need for a pressing cloth with synthetic fabrics. It keeps the hot metal soleplate from direct contact with fabric, and can be used with steam or dry iron. Be sure to test press your fabric in any case.

The preceding charts give general rules for pressing fabrics. There are two parts. You will need to consult both because either or both fiber and fabric construction may require or restrict heat, moisture, or other conditions. This will determine how to press your fabric, but it is not a substitute for test pressing.

To use the chart as a guide, use all the procedures for pressing fiber or fabric construction by standard method (black circles and type) or an alternate method (colored circles and type). Colored and black circles in a single square indicate a procedure used in both methods. Try method on a scrap of fabric.

96

You can approach making your shirt in two different ways. If you have not had real fitting problems in other patterns or in ready-to-wear, you can usually begin right away with your garment fabric. If you have had difficulty finding a good fit, especially in your shoulders and torso, you will want to pretest your garment in an inexpensive fabric, preferably a woven check or plaid. (Either will help you to see the crosswise and lengthwise grain of your garment; both are very useful when fitting.)

This is because a fitting problem in shoulders or torso may require cutting a garment piece differently. If the fashion fabric has already been cut when this is learned, you will have made an expensive mistake.

Both approaches follow the same steps. First, use the instructions under Pattern Adjustments (next section) to compare your measurements with those of the pattern. Where they differ, you can make simple adjustments for length or girth. Then, cut your garment (either from the fashion fabric or your trial fabric), incorporating the necessary pattern adjustments. Add ½ inch (1.3cm) beyond the regular seam allowance on each side seam to allow for simple fitting. You will baste on the regulation seamline.

The next step will be fitting the garment. (Instructions follow Pattern Adjustments.) Here, procedures for making the trial garment and the fashion garment differ. In the latter you can make simple adjustments by taking up or letting out seams and darts as necessary to fit the garment to the figure. You can make these minor changes in the trial garment, too, but you also should study the garment to learn how to adjust for such problems as broad shoulders or a large neck base. From adjustments made on the trial garment you will learn how to pivot or shift the pattern when cutting your fashion garment. The fitted trial shirt can also be used to make a master pattern, from which you can make all types of shirts. Instructions for a master pattern are given at the end of the fitting section.

PATTERN ADJUSTMENTS

Pattern alterations always follow certain basic principles. Complete respect for grainline is essential. There are four ways to adjust patterns and maintain the grainline. Two adjustments are made within the pattern before cutting. Two are made during cutting (cutting-to-fit). The methods are illustrated in the following pages.

PIN AN EVEN TUCK To shorten a pattern or decrease its width, an even tuck can be pinned on lengthwise or crosswise grain. Always remember to straighten the pattern edge across folded tucks.

SLASH AND ADD TISSUE To lengthen or increase pattern width, the pattern can be cut apart on lengthwise or crosswise grain, and tissue inserted and fastened with tape.

Using colored tissue will make it easier to see pattern adjustments.

Be sure to straighten any seamlines that have been made uneven by either length adjustment.

SLIDE THE PATTERN When an entire side of a pattern requires an addition in length or width, slide the pattern as follows. Lay pattern piece on fabric; pin in place. Allow enough space on fabric to slide the pattern. Cut area of pattern piece that does not need alteration. Mark extra amount needed with chalk on fabric. (If this is in girth, only one-fourth should be added to each side seam allowance.) Unpin and slide pattern to chalk marks, pin in position, and complete cutting. Return pattern to original position to mark.

PIVOT THE PATTERN To add to a portion of the length or width of a pattern (the waist area, for example), pivot the pattern as follows. Lay pattern on fabric; pin in place. Cut around pattern in area that does not need alteration. Measure and chalk mark the additional amount of fabric needed. (For width, add one-fourth of total to each side seam allowance.) Partially unpin pattern, and pivot a corner to chalk-marked position. Pin pattern, and complete cutting. Return pattern to original position for marking.

When a pattern piece requires several adjustments, lay it on colored tissue as you would on fabric. Mark areas needing alteration, slide and/or pivot as required to make necessary changes, cut out colored tissue, and fasten pattern to tissue with transparent tape.

If you use this method to make your pattern adjustments you will find it easy to make a master pattern for shirts or shirt garments. You will want to wait until your garment has been basted and fitted to see if any further alterations are necessary; make these changes with colored tissue also. Instructions for making a master pattern are given at the end of the fitting section, page 112.

ADDING A BUST DART TO A SHIRT PATTERN

If your pattern does not have a bust dart and you need one for a perfect fit, you can add a dart from another pattern that fits you well. To accurately reproduce the dart, you must draw it not only the same size as the original, but also the same distance below the armhole and at the same angle to lengthwise grain.

When you trace the dart you will probably need to add tissue at the side of the pattern in order to trace the shape of the dart at the side seamline (the jog). Tape a piece of tissue paper from the underarm edge down past the area where the dart will be.

Place the shirt-style pattern over the darted pattern with the lengthwise grain markings exactly aligned. Slide the shirt pattern until the lower edges of the patterns' armholes are perfectly keyed. Be sure that the lengthwise grain markings remain parallel to each other. Trace the dart, using a straight edge and a soft colored pencil. Extend the lines into the tissue as necessary to create the proper shape at the side seam. To make sure your dart is traced correctly, draw in a pickup line (dividing the dart in two), and fold the pattern, pinning the dart in place. The side seamline should form a smooth line. If not, the jog is not drawn correctly.

Add an amount of tissue as deep as the widest part of dart across the lower edge of the shirt front, to key the side seams of front and back.

LENGTH ADJUSTMENTS

The length of your garment may be changed either through the body of the garment or at the lower edge. You can make the entire alteration at the lower edge (which is easier) unless your shirt garment is very closely fitted.

3 TO LENGTHEN   Add the necessary amount to the lower edge of the pattern. To retain the shape of the pattern edge, measure every few inches across it. Adjust both front and back in the same way.

4 TO SHORTEN   Remove the necessary amount from the pattern at the lower edge. Measure and mark the

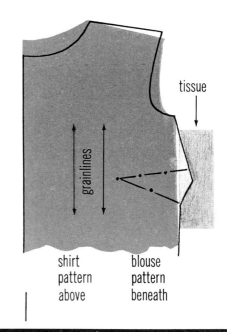

grainlines

tissue

shirt
pattern
above

blouse
pattern
beneath

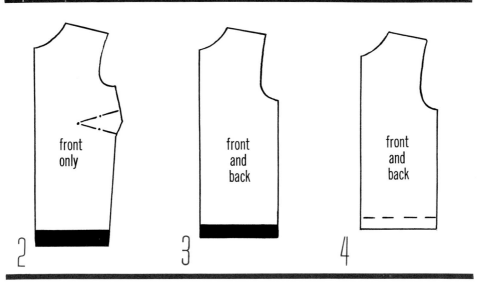

front
only

front
and
back

front
and
back

2   3   4

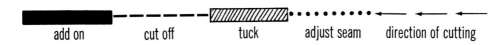

add on   cut off   tuck   adjust seam   direction of cutting

correct length on the pattern every few inches above the hemline to maintain the original shape of the pattern. Adjust front and back.

TO ALTER GARMENT FITTED AT WAISTLINE For an adjustment of 2 inches (5cm) or less, add or remove length at the lower edge as described. If the garment needs to be lengthened more than 2 inches (5cm), add the remainder by slashing the adjustment line and inserting a piece of colored tissue the necessary depth. Adjust both front and back in the same way. If the garment needs to be shortened more than 2 inches (5cm), measure the rest to be removed, and draw a line that distance above the adjustment line. Fold the pattern accurately on the adjustment line, and bring the fold up to the second line. Pin or tape in place. Adjust both back and front.

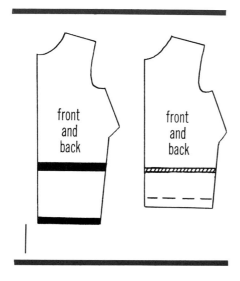

NECKLINE ADJUSTMENTS

Measure your neck and add ½ inch (1.3cm) for comfort ease. Check the total against the pattern neck measurement. Men will find this measurement given on the pattern envelope. Women will have to measure around the neckline of the pattern pieces with a tape measure standing on edge. To get total circumference, remember to double the measure of a pattern piece to be placed on fold or cut twice.

TO INCREASE NECKLINE If your comparison shows that the pattern neckline is too small, you should wait to fix it until you have cut out the garment and basted it for a fitting. You will not want to cut the neckline larger now, because it may fit differently around your neck than the measure indicates. Also, if the neckline is too tight, the tightness may be only in front, only in back, or only at the shoulder seams. The basted garment will indicate which of these is the problem, and you can alter it accordingly. Instructions are given in Fitting. Always wait to cut collar until neckline is fitted.

TO DECREASE NECKLINE If you find that the garment neckline might be too large, you should add extra fabric to decrease the neckline as you cut. You certainly cannot add it later unless you are making a trial garment. Even then, it is probably better to have the extra fabric to work with so you can see exactly how much will be needed when you make your fashion garment. Add on to both front and back neckline. Adding ⅛ inch (3mm) all around the

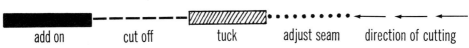

| add on | cut off | tuck | adjust seam | direction of cutting |

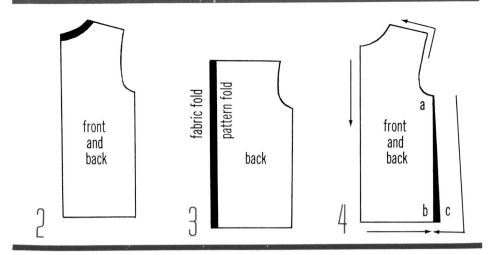

neckline will decrease its size about ½ inch (1.3cm). Wait to cut the collar until the neckline has been fitted.

BODY OF PATTERN

Measure your hips at their fullest part. Compare this measure with the hip measurement given for your size on the pattern envelope. Alteration may be needed on the pattern back only or in total hip girth.

WIDE BACK OR HIPS In a shirt with a back yoke, width may be added below the yoke by laying the pattern a distance one-half the required addition from the fabric fold before cutting. (Since the alteration is made at the fold, the piece will be increased by twice the distance between fold and pattern.) When you stitch the back to the yoke, the extra fullness is placed in tucks or gathers toward the armhole edges. See Shirt Construction.

TO INCREASE GIRTH AT HIPLINE As much as 1 inch (2.5cm) can be added to each side seam, front and back pattern pieces, for a total of 4 inches (10cm). Pin pattern to fabric, and cut from **a** to **b** as shown. (Do not cut along a pattern foldline.) At side seamline, measure and mark amount to be added at hipline, **c.** The addition should taper to original seamline below armhole. Unpin pattern, and pivot to **c.** Pin, and cut between **c** and **a.**

Return pattern to original position to transfer markings. Adjust front and back pattern pieces in the same way. If additional amount is not needed at waistline, remove it by increasing seams when you are fitting garment. Do not fit the garment too tightly at the hipline.

TO DECREASE GIRTH AT HIPLINE Cut fabric without adjusting pattern width. Excess fabric can be removed, one-fourth of the amount from each side seamline, after the dress has been fitted. Instructions for taking up seams are given in Fitting.

SLEEVE LENGTH

A traditional shirt sleeve has fairly consistent ease throughout and its

101

pattern usually has only one adjustment line for lengthening and shortening. However, some blouse and dress patterns have a closer fitting sleeve with darts at the elbow. These usually have two adjustment lines — one above the elbow and one below. For a shirt sleeve measure the length of your arm from shoulder joint to wrist with arm bent. Measure the sleeve pattern to what will be the lower edge of finished hem or cuff. Then compare the measurements to see if adjustment is needed.

For a sleeve with two adjustment lines, measure in two steps — one from shoulder to elbow, the other from elbow to wrist. Also measure the pattern in two steps. Compare the two sets of measurements. The sleeve may require lengthening above or below the elbow darts or in both places.

If a man knows that the sleeve length given for his pattern size is the same as his ready-to-wear size or his actual sleeve length (see illustration) he need not check the pattern sleeve and arm measurements. He should not compare arm length and "sleeve length." As you can see they are different.

TO SHORTEN A LONG SLEEVE Figure the amount to be shortened and mark the distance from the adjustment line(s). Draw a straight line through your marks. Fold on adjustment line(s) and bring fold(s) to your line(s). Pin or tape in place.

TO LENGTHEN A LONG SLEEVE Figure the amount needed. Slash the pattern at adjustment line(s), and insert amount of tissue required. Fasten with tape.

TO SHORTEN OR LENGTHEN A SHORT SLEEVE Depending on style, a short sleeve may usually be lengthened or shortened at the lower edge.

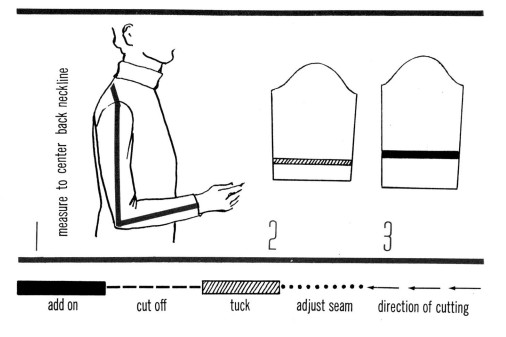

| add on | cut off | tuck | adjust seam | direction of cutting |

STANDARDS FOR CUSTOM FITTING

Your shirt should be fitted carefully. Attention to this step of construction is essential if your investment of labor in the other steps — fabric preparation, cutting, marking, stitching, and pressing — is to pay dividends.

After adjusting your pattern and cutting the garment, follow the instructions in General Construction and Shirt Front Units to baste it for fitting. Stitch on the regulation seamline. (The extra width added to the seam allowances will not be used unless necessary in fitting.) Sleeves can be basted into armholes (see instructions for attaching sleeves) and the side and underarm seams basted, but you will not need to finish the sleeve with a placket or cuff. Do fold the cuff and pin it to the sleeve to check total length, however. The collar should be cut after the neckline has been fitted. If neckline alterations are involved, the neckline of the collar will have to be altered to match that of the garment.

Standards for custom fitting should, of course, be applied to a garment cut from fashion fabric as well as to a trial garment. In a trial garment they will show the pattern adjustments and fitting alterations that will be necessary when you cut your fashion fabric. In a fashion garment the standards will indicate minor changes needed to perfect the fit. When you have basted your garment, try it on and check the following areas before a full-length mirror.

SHOULDERS Unless your pattern has an extended shoulderline, the shoulder seam should fall exactly on the crest of the shoulder and lie smoothly from shoulder joint to neckline. The shoulder seam on shirts with set-in or shirt sleeves should end at the shoulder joint.

NECKLINE AND COLLAR The neckline should lie smoothly and comfortably at the base of the neck. Wait to cut the collar until the neckline has been fitted. If fitting the neckline is necessary, see neckline and collar alterations, page 104. Baste your collar together according to instructions for the type you are making, and baste it to the neckline.

The depth and shape of the collar is important because it is worn so close to the face. The outside edges of a collar easily can be modified to flatter your face and neck. The height of the collar and neckband should be proportionate to the length of your neck. The collar should lie smoothly at the base of your neck. A collar with a neckband (a two-piece collar) will look and fit better than a one-piece collar.

BUST A woman with a B or larger size bust cup will need a bust dart in a shirt just as she does in any other garment because darts give the necessary shape.

If your pattern has bust darts, they should point to the apex of the bust. Darts should end ½ to 1 inch (1.3 to 2.5cm) from the apex, the area of the greatest shape. Sometimes you will need to shorten darts. The greater the width of a dart, the more shape is created beyond the dart point. Figures with small curves will require shallow darts. Very rounded figures usually require one or more fairly deep darts at the bust.

SLEEVES The arm should not touch or distort the line of the sleeve at any point. Pin the folded cuff to the sleeve to check both sleeve length and the proportion of the cuff to the depth of the sleeve. The cuff edge or hemline of a long sleeve should fall at the point the hand joins the wrist. (To measure the correct length of a long sleeve, bend your elbow.)

Short sleeves should be the length most attractive for your arm. A short sleeve may extend to the bend of the elbow. Bright-colored fabrics attract more attention to the arm than colors that blend with the skin tone.

SLEEVELESS ARMHOLES The armhole should not gap. If it does, it is too large. The underarm seam should be no more than 1 inch (2.5cm) below the armpit in a garment with sleeves. It may need to be higher than this in a sleeveless garment. If the armhole is too small, it will pull and bind. Determine how much will need to be added or removed from the pattern to make the armhole both attractive and comfortable to wear.

SHIRT LENGTH Shirts worn outside pants, shirt tunics, or shirt jackets are far more flattering to the figure when they are long enough to cover the crotch seam. The only exception is when this length is disproportionate for a person with very short legs. Unless a shirt is to be worn tucked in, there should be enough length to permit a 1½ to 2-inch (3.8 to 5-cm) hem. A 1-inch (2.5-cm) hem is desirable for men's shirts.

FITTING BY SIMPLE SEAM ADJUSTMENTS

After basting your garment and trying it on, you may find that one or more seams must be taken up. You will pin the seams on the outside to take them up because you will try on the garment right side out. To transfer the new seamline to the wrong side of the garment for stitching, turn the garment to the wrong

side, and rub tailor's chalk along the pinned seam as shown. If any seams must be let out, the amount of additions needed will be determined by opening the seams and pinning them as desired.

FITTING NECKLINE AND COLLAR

TO INCREASE NECKLINE Cut neckline larger as necessary by trimming excess in a smooth line. You may want the increase only in front, only in back, or only at the shoulder seams. Trim accordingly, always following the shape of the pattern and tapering gradually if you return to the original seamline.

COLLAR The collar must be altered to match the neckline. If you increase the neckline, add a corresponding amount to the center back of the collar (and neckband if it is a separate piece). To determine the amount you need to add, pin the pattern to the neckline, or cut a collar from inexpensive fabric and use it. If the center back of the pattern is to be placed on fold, simply move it out one half the amount required from the fabric fold. If the piece is to be cut in a single layer, slash it vertically and insert a strip of tissue equal to the amount required. Tape in place.

If you have decreased the neckline (in Pattern Adjustments) remove a corresponding amount from the center back of the collar (and neckband if it is a separate piece). To determine the amount you need to remove, fit the neckline carefully, trimming it if necessary, and pin to it the collar pattern or a collar cut from inexpensive fabric. If the center back of the pattern is to be placed on fold, simply trim off half the amount you wish to remove. If the piece is to be cut in a single layer, fold an even,

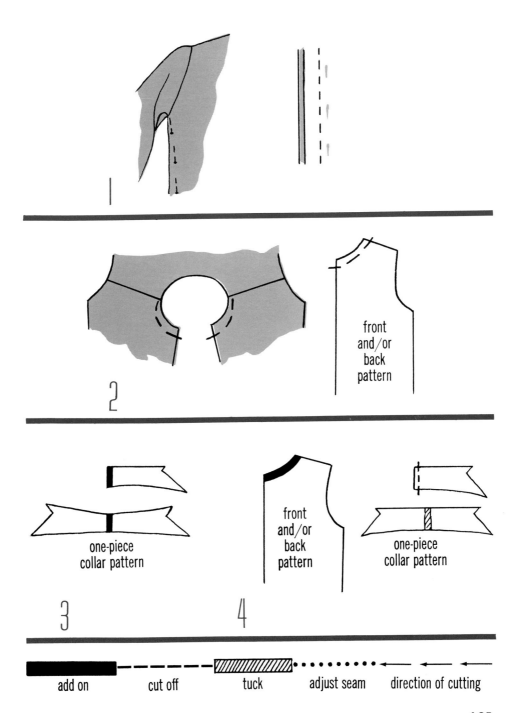

1

2

front
and/or
back
pattern

3

one-piece
collar pattern

4

front
and/or
back
pattern

one-piece
collar pattern

add on   cut off   tuck   adjust seam   direction of cutting

vertical tuck at center back of pattern the width you wish to remove.

You can figure that if you trim off or add on ⅛ inch (3mm) all around the neckline, you will be changing its girth by about ½ inch (1.3cm). Then when you add or subtract from the collar pattern, you would use ½ inch (1.3cm) for a piece to be cut in a single layer and ¼ inch (6mm) for a piece to be cut on fold. These measurements cannot be exact because a neckline is not a perfect circle.

DEPTH OF NECKBAND Using the pattern or trial fabric, try on the neckband and collar. If the neckband seems too high for the neck, fold an even tuck on true grain of pattern before cutting the fashion fabric. A ⅛-inch (3-mm) tuck will decrease the height ¼ inch (6mm). If the neckband seems too narrow for the neck, slash pattern, and add the desired amount in colored tissue on true grain of pattern before pinning to fashion fabric.

KEY GRAINLINES

Alterations for repositioning bust darts, if any, and some shoulder alterations will be based on the key grainline, so-called because they are keys to fitting your garment. When the fabric has been made grain-perfect you can use the key grainlines for fitting.

When the garment fits properly, the keys will lie as shown in the illustration. This will be easy to determine if your trial fabric is a woven check or plaid. If the keys are not in the position shown, the garment requires further fitting. There are other keys for other garments, but for shirt fitting you need only those shown: on the back, shoulder and underarm; on the front, chest and, for women,

bust. The chest grainline lies about 4½ inches (11.5cm) below shoulderline on crosswise grain. Bust grainline lies across crown of bust on crosswise grain. Shoulder grainline is about 4½ inches (11.5cm) below shoulderline on crosswise grain, and underarm is about 1½ inches (3.8cm) below armhole, across shoulders on crosswise grain.

FITTING THE SHOULDERS

Perfect fit at the shoulders is vital to the good looks of your garment. Not only does shoulder fit affect the hang of the garment lower down, but in a shirt style the shoulder area often is the only place the garment is really fitted to the figure.

NARROW SHOULDERS The garment seam extends beyond the shoulder joint. To correct pattern, cut front shoulderline shorter at armhole as far in as the straight of lengthwise grain, tapering to original seamline at front notch of armhole. Or, if there is a princess or fitted seam, deepen it at the shoulderline, tapering it to the original seamline (for women, above the apex of the bust). If there is no seam, a woman with a large bust should use a dart or several tucks at the shoulderline. Fit each shoulder carefully. Sometimes one shoulder is narrower than the other.

To match the front and back shoulder seams, increase the width of the dart in the back shoulderline, or add a narrow dart if there is none. For larger figures, especially, easing the back to the front will give the best fit. Do not cut off the armhole in both front and back; the sleeve would not hang true.

BROAD SHOULDERS The sleeves pull up on the shoulders. The armhole seam falls above the shoulder joint, on the shoulderline. Wrinkles

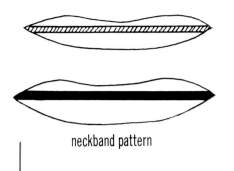

neckband pattern

1

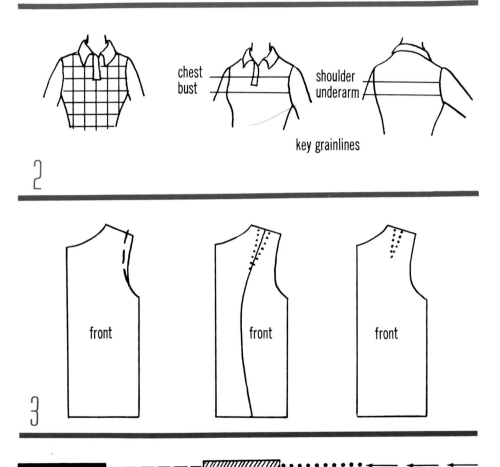

chest
bust

shoulder
underarm

key grainlines

2

front

front

front

3

add on   cut off   tuck   adjust seam   direction of cutting

107

may appear across the chest. More fabric will be needed on both back and front at the upper armhole.

Pin pattern to fabric, and cut from **a** to **b,** at armhole notch. Do not cut along a foldline. Mark the addition needed at **c.** Unpin pattern, and pivot at **b,** moving **a** to **c.** Pin, and complete cutting at armhole. Return pattern to original position to mark.

SLOPING SHOULDERS The garment sags in the underarm area. This is a common alteration for a sleeveless garment.

For a garment cut from fashion fabric, pin garment from shoulder to fit, tapering to original seam at neckline. For a trial garment do the same; then pin pattern to fashion fabric, and cut from **a** to **b,** as shown. Do not cut along a pattern foldline. Mark **c,** the amount pinned out at shoulder on trial garment. Pivot on **b** to **c.** Pin, and cut between **b** and **c.** Unpin, place shoulder of pattern at **c,** and keep lengthwise grain of pattern true. Pin, and cut armhole between **c** and **a.** Return pattern to original position to transfer markings. Alter both back and front.

SQUARE SHOULDERS Wrinkles form across the back beneath the neck. There is strain on shoulder and armhole seams, and they will be pulled off grain. This is a grainline problem. Study the key grainline illustrations. The key shoulder grainline swings up as it nears the armhole. This alteration may be done only on the back, but it is done more frequently on both front and back of a garment.

To correct, let out shoulder seam until grainline is straight. Try to see if alteration is needed on both front and back, or only on back. Measure amounts let out at shoulder, both

height and width. To alter pattern do this: Pin pattern to fabric, and cut from **a** to **b.** Do not cut along a pattern foldline. Mark addition needed at armhole, **c,** and addition needed in height at shoulder seam, **d.** Unpin pattern, and pivot on **b** to **d.** Pin, and cut between **b** and **d.** Unpin, and slide pattern up to **d,** keeping pattern on true lengthwise grain. Complete cutting armhole between **d** and **a.** Return pattern to original position to mark.

To correct only pattern back, add to back only, as described in preceding paragraph. The back can be matched to the front at the shoulder seams by increasing the width of the back shoulder darts, by making two back shoulder darts, or by using ease plus to ease the back of the shoulder to the front. Facings and collars should be cut to match the altered shoulderline of garment.

ROUND SHOULDERS The back of the shirt will be too tight across the upper shoulders and will be pulled up so it is shorter at center back. The shoulder key grainline swings up as it approaches center back. Fitting problem is a combination of Thick Base of Neck, and Broad Shoulders:

Step 1. Pin pattern to fabric, and cut from **a** to **b.** Do not cut along a pattern foldline. Mark **d,** the amount needed to increase the shoulder width. Pivot on **b** to **d,** and cut, tapering to original position at **b.**

Step 2. Mark amount of increase (**f** and **c**) needed at pattern neck edges **a** and **e.** Unpin pattern, and slide it so **a** and **e** meet **f** and **c.** Cut between **c** and **f** and **d.** Return pattern to original position for marking.

To match front and back shoulder seams increase the back shoulder dart or add one the same amount as was added to armhole. A shortened curved dart is used for round shoulders. The curved dart is stitched with an inside curve to give more fabric where it is needed.

THICK BASE OF NECK AND UPPER SHOULDERS This problem begins at the base of the neck and extends into the upper shoulderline. It may occur on front only, back only, both front and back, or on one shoulder only. The grainline will indicate which of these is the problem.

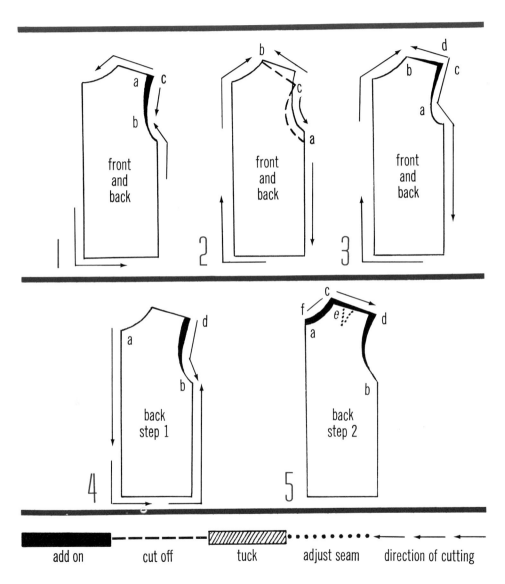

add on   cut off   tuck   adjust seam   direction of cutting

The garment pulls from neckline to underarm, forming wrinkles in these areas. The hemline will be shorter at center front, center back, or both.

When the problem is with both back and front, as shown here, the key grainlines swing up in the center. If you hold a tape measure straight across the back or front between points where the key grainline intersects with the arms, you will see how much the grainline swings up. This is the amount that must be added to the shoulder seam at the neckline to correct the problem.

To correct, pin pattern to fabric, and cut from **b** to **a.** Do not cut on a foldline. Mark **c** to indicate the amount needed at neckline shoulder seam to correct the key grainline. Unpin pattern, and pivot on **a** to bring neck edge to **c.** Pin in place, and cut from **a** to **c.** To cut neck edge, slide pattern up to **c,** keeping it on grain. Cut neckline from **c** to **b.** Return pattern to original position and transfer markings. When you try on the garment, you may find that the neck edge needs to be lowered at

center front or center back. When this has been determined, cut collar and facings the same way.

ADJUSTING BUST DART POSITION

Make any necessary shoulder alterations before adjusting underarm darts. The underarm dart must point directly to the apex (crown) of the bust and stop 1 to ½ inch (2.5 to 1.3cm) from it. The following methods of alteration retain the slanted line of the dart, which gives it a pleasing appearance.

A trial garment will show you the amount the dart needs to be raised or lowered. Then you can make the necessary alteration when cutting out your fashion fabric. If the bust dart is too low, the bust key grainline will drop below the crown of the bust, and there will be a bulge under the bust at the point of the dart. If the bust dart is too high, the key grainline will ride over the crown of the bust. There will be a bulge at the point of the dart.

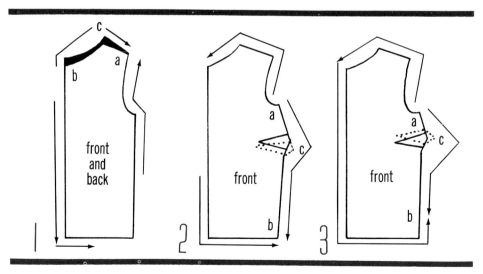

TO LOWER DART Pin pattern to fabric, and cut from **a** to **b.** (**A** should be about 1 inch below armhole.) Do not cut along a foldline. Mark **c,** the point to which the pickup line of dart is to be lowered. Unpin, and slide pattern down until pattern pickup line is at **c.** Keep pattern on true grain. Pin and cut remainder of side seam from **a** to **b.** Transfer dart markings to fabric while pattern is in this position.

TO RAISE DART Pin pattern on fabric, and cut from **a** to **b.** (**B** should be about 2 inches (5cm) above waistline.) Do not cut along a foldline. Mark **c,** the position of corrected pickup line. Unpin pattern, and raise so pickup line of pattern dart coincides with **c.** Keep pattern on true lengthwise grainline. Pin, and cut from **a** to **b.** Transfer dart markings. Repin pattern to original position to transfer any other markings.

FITTING SLEEVES

SLEEVECAP If there is too much ease in the sleevecap for the look you desire, it can be decreased.

1. A small, slender dart in the center of the sleevecap will give it a flatter look.
2. An even tuck can be taken in the pattern to remove the necessary amount. A ⅛-inch (3-mm) tuck on true grain will decrease the cap ½ inch (1.3cm). If very much ease is removed from the cap, the sleeve may need to be cut wider at the lower edge for comfort. If you have already cut your sleeve from fashion fabric, simply place the tucked pattern over it and recut the cap. In this case, be careful not to remove too much ease, because the width you can add at the lower edge is limited to the seam allowances, 1 inch (2.5cm) at most.

Additional ease and length of sleeve-cap can be obtained by slashing the sleeve pattern between sleevecap notches and inserting tissue one-fourth the amount of the total addition desired. This will add to the fullness of the sleevecap, because the ease will need to be increased in order to fit sleeve to armhole.

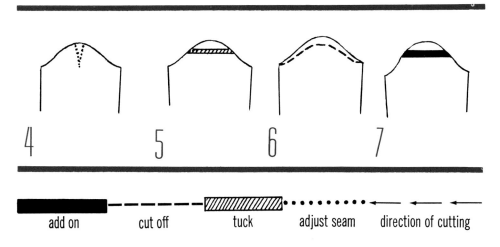

| add on | cut off | tuck | adjust seam | direction of cutting |

SLEEVE WIDTH   A sleeve that seems too full can be tapered in at the sides as shown. If more fullness is desired it can be added as shown. Both techniques may also be used on fashion fabric if your sleeve is already cut, but the amount you can add will, of course, be limited by the width of the seam allowance.

MAKING A MASTER PATTERN

If you followed the suggestion on page 98 to make all adjustments directly on your pattern with tissue paper, you are ready to make a master. If you have made a trial garment and need to transfer some adjustments from the trial garment to the pattern you should follow directions in the next paragraphs.

TO TRANSFER ADJUSTMENTS   To transfer alterations from the trial garment to the pattern you will need to take the trial garment apart after all adjustments have been made on it and it has been fitted perfectly. All seamlines should be trimmed to ⅝ inch (1.5cm).

THE MASTER   When you have made all adjustments on the pattern tissue (either by transferring as above or by adjusting the pattern as you work), make your master pattern by either of the following methods:

1. Trace the adjusted pattern pieces on heavyweight nonwoven interfacing, brown wrapping paper, or a product made for tracing patterns. Transfer all adjusted pattern markings, and redraw seamlines as necessary for your alterations.
2. After adjusting pattern pieces and redrawing markings and seamlines as necessary, lay the pieces on iron-on nonwoven interfacing fabric, and press pieces carefully to the fabric. Then cut them out.

Fabric can affect the fit of a pattern. Take this into account when using your master pattern—allow a slightly wider side seam allowance when cutting so you will be able to make any necessary adjustments during fitting. Record on the master or in a notebook changes necessary for fitting different fabrics.

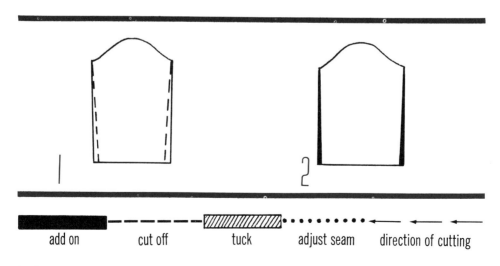

add on   cut off   tuck   adjust seam   direction of cutting

114

115